Canadian Folk

Canadian Folk
Portraits of Remarkable Lives

Peter Unwin

DUNDURN
TORONTO

Editor: Shannon Whibbs
Design: Jennifer Scott
Printer: Webcom

Library and Archives Canada Cataloguing in Publication

Unwin, Peter, 1956-, author
        Canadian folk : portraits of remarkable lives / by Peter Unwin.

Issued in print and electronic formats.
ISBN 978-1-4597-1027-6 (pbk.).--ISBN 978-1-4597-1028-3 (pdf).--ISBN 978-1-4597-1029-0 (epub)

        1. Canada--Biography. I. Title.

FC25.U68 2013   971.009'9   C2013-900903-5   C2013-900904-3

1   2   3   4   5   17   16   15   14   13

We acknowledge the support of the Canada Council for the Arts and the Ontario Arts Council for our publishing program. We also acknowledge the financial support of the Government of Canada through the Canada Book Fund and Livres Canada Books, and the Government of Ontario through the Ontario Book Publishing Tax Credit and the Ontario Media Development Corporation.

Care has been taken to trace the ownership of copyright material used in this book. The author and the publisher welcome any information enabling them to rectify any references or credits in subsequent editions.

J. Kirk Howard, President

Printed and bound in Canada.

Visit us at
Dundurn.com | @dundurnpress | Facebook.com/dundurnpress | Pinterest.com/dundurnpress

Dundurn
3 Church Street, Suite 500
Toronto, Ontario, Canada
M5E 1M2

Gazelle Book Services Limited
White Cross Mills
High Town, Lancaster, England
LA1 4XS

Dundurn
2250 Military Road
Tonawanda, NY
U.S.A. 14150

Contents

Introduction

In writing and researching *Canadian Folk*, I was perhaps fortunate to arrive at no conclusive insights into Canada or Canadians. What I repeatedly encountered was the notion that "to be" Canadian, or to attempt to qualify as one, involved travelling great distances by canoe, by train, or boat, on foot, by dogsled, by snowshoe, or any combination of the above. Frequently this travel was undertaken during a blinding snowstorm or in a sinking ship, in which the captain was drunk and probably the ship was on fire.

More often than not the people who inhabit *Canadian Folk* were marked by a noticeable inability to sit still. They were perpetually northbound or south; they were inveterate walkers, or world-class runners, millionaires in ill-advised Citroën half tracks. The restless characters who spanned those miles, and who fill the pages of this book, were fuelled by the ambitions, the doubts, and the certainties of their times, a certainty that now seems unfathomable to us and frequently maddening.

More than a few started out fascinated by the forest and what they hoped was the redemptive power of the wilderness and a

Native way of life. Some were Native themselves, or wanted to be, or tried to be, and did not fit easily into the book of history. Some were celebrated or reviled around the world, some were clubbed to death on remote islands, some were hateful, others sublime in their decency and manners.

Many of the people in this book left extensive records of their passing in the form of poems, letters, books, or paintings. Some of them painted on ancient rock using a form of paint that defies science. All of them travelled through the vast kingdoms of the Native gods of North America, whose names were often unpronounceable and unknown to them. A few had the responsibility of watching entire ways of life vanish before their eyes.

Today we know them by their vitality of their existence, or sometimes by the damage they left behind. More often, and increasingly, we don't know them at all.

1

"A Misserable Barren Place"

The year of his birth is not known. It is usually approximated around 1640, although recent evidence uncovered in New England may force the date forward. The year of his death is not known, either. It would seem he died under mysterious and extremely grim circumstances on Marble Island, twenty-five miles off Rankin Inlet, in 1720, or 1721. Even what he looked like is unknown, there being no portrait painted, or none that has passed into history. What evidence there is suggests a man who left behind a legacy of resentfulness, jealousy, almost unbelievable hard work, and suffering; a grim, humourless character who, for half a century, dominated the lower half of Hudson Bay.

What is known of James Knight is that in 1676 he entered the service of the Hudson's Bay Company already a mature man and a shipwright by trade. In this same year or shortly after, following an ocean voyage that lasted eighty days, he entered, for the first time, the ferocious "Western Sea" of Hudson's Bay. His assignment was to build or rebuild the Company's forts and factories at the "Bottom of the Baye." Of this first encounter he would write tellingly forty years later: "It has been My Misfortune Always to have Nothing but Fatigue and Trouble in this Countree, for when I first came into it wee had Nothing but a little place not fitt to keep Hoggs in."

For some reason no amount of Fatigue and Trouble could keep James Knight out of this "Countree." By 1682 he was outfitted for a return voyage, this time as deputy governor. It is typical of the man's abrasive relationship with almost everyone that on the day the expedition was to sail, the London-based Committee of the Hudson's Bay Company, concerned that Knight would engage in private trade, refused him the right to board the ships. Somehow the conflict was resolved and he sailed the same day.

As second-in-command, Knight served under Governor John Nixon, a "tetchy," "sanctimonious" "disappointment" who excused his own fondness for liquor on the grounds that "Water doth not agree with me." His own men were said to be appalled by his savage treatment of the Natives. Perhaps it is telling that this is one of the very few men with whom James Knight did not clash.

These relations changed when Nixon was replaced as governor by Henry Sergeant. Hand-picked by the Duke of York, Sergeant had "pertaining to him" "a parcel of women:" his wife, her friend, and a maidservant, the first white women to winter in Hudson's Bay. Almost immediately the new governor directed charges against Knight, likely to the effect that Knight was packing out "skins" for private sale. Returning to England in 1685, Knight dodged these charges by proposing a scheme to reduce the costs of maintaining outposts at the Bottom of the Bay. He also produced testimonials to his character which, in his own mind, exonerated him. In the minds of the Committee, however, James Knight was not to be trusted and there followed a seven-year absence from Company employment. During this time, the reputation of Henry Sergeant fell dramatically when he surrendered Albany Fort to the French without a fight. It is said his wife fainted at the first shot and the rest of the English garrison retreated into a cellar and cowered there. For this "ill Conduct, perfidiousness & Cowardize," the Company presented the disgraced governor with a bill for £20,000. Despite a lengthy court battle, they never collected.

In 1692, James Knight was back in favour and granted the title of "Governor & Commander in Cheif of all and every of Our Forts Factory's Lands and Territory with the dependencys contained and lying in ye bottome of the Bay ... commonly called Hudson's Streights in America." In 1693, he led a powerful force into Hudson's Bay and retook Albany Fort from the French. After a furious first fusillade, Knight discovered the fort empty but for a prisoner clapped in irons. The man, quite insane, had murdered the French surgeon and stove in the chaplain's head with an axe.

Knight remained on as governor at the Bottom of the Baye until 1697, before sailing for England. He returned the following year, but finally in 1700 sailed for England, apparently for good.

At this point, James Knight possessed nearly twenty-five years of experience in one of the harshest environments on the planet. It was a land where vinegar froze solid and had to be chopped with a hatchet. "Good port wine froze in the glass as pour'd out of the Bottle," and a red hot cannonball weighing twenty-four pounds hung next to a glass window could not keep it from freezing overnight. When summer finally came, so did the sucking insects. The terror that these creatures brought with them is apparent on almost every page of Knight's diaries: "Musketos & horse flies ... Swarms of Small Sand flyes wch is worst of all ...

wee can hardly see the Sun through them ... Our Hands and face is nothing but Scabbs." At times it was not possible for Knight or his men to even open their mouths. A twentieth-century study in this area found an exposed person subject to ten thousand bites per hour.

Men like Knight and his crews who came to this part of the world were attempting to survive in a region where even skilled Cree and Chipewyan hunters routinely starved. It was here that the Danish expedition led by Jens Munk in 1619 lost sixty of sixty-three men (amazingly, the three survivors somehow sailed back to Europe). Natives arriving the following summer encoun-- tered so many corpses that they fled in terror. It was land literally scattered with the bones of European adventurers, so much so that when Knight began construction on Churchill fort in 1717, his crew actually dug on the skeletons of those Danish sailors who had died in the previous century.

It was also land that Governor James Knight apparently despised from the depths of his heart. "I never knowd no place so troublesom as this is here," he wrote. "This is a Misserable barren Place" ... "York Fort is badd but this is Tenn times worse ... for here is neither fish, Fowl nor Venison." *For here is nether fish fowl nor Venison.* This phrase repeats like a coda through the man's diaries and begs the question, why? Why spend more than half his life here, why keep coming back, building crude forts on the bones of the men who had perished before him? Knight was far from a young man, the vigour and the pains of this place took their toll on his body by the hour. And yet he returned. Even as a gentleman of wealth and comfort, without obvious need of a wage, he returned and kept returning until in the end, he disappeared altogether.

It is possible that in the barren and dark boreal stretches of Hudson's Bay, James Knight encountered a landscape that he could not resist. There are such regions that tug at the imagination, that haunt the memory and will not let go. But beyond a fleeting, even charming, description of the Northern Lights, which he described as the "Petty Dancers," likely a misspelling of "pretty," he displayed no poetic fascination with the land, no interest at all beyond the countless diary notes on this "Misserable barren Place (where) Wee hardly See a Goose … nor never a fish."

It is more likely that the glinting seduction of gold had already entered James Knight's imagination. We are told that the discovery of minerals, gold in particular, "was always his Topic." Henry Kelsey, who would a play a role in Knight's grim demise, contemptuously referred to the man as "the Goldfinder." Constantly grilling the surrounding Natives for the location of the precious "yellow mettle," it was reported he "knew his way to this place as well as to his bedside," and did not go anywhere without his "Cruseables, Melting Potts, Borax &c for the trial of Minerals." Even in his diary, when the subject of minerals comes up, he turns suddenly poetic: "Great Virgin Copper lumps of it so bigg that 3 or 4 men can't lift it." When a Native woman claimed to have seen deposits of gold on a western coastline, Knight confided, breathlessly, "Her eyes had seen it and her hands hadd fellt it."

This is the general historical consensus on James Knight; a Goldfinder, a man smitten by the lure of precious metals, one of the first Englishmen to die in a futile and life-long search for gold. But there are perhaps other threads that make up the man. There is the reality of the landscape itself, situated on the very perimeter of the known world. In this remote land, James Knight was no longer an anonymous English "gentleman." He was instead a type of king. His words, his actions, his decisions were carried out as law. With a simple command he changed age-old Native social arrangements and trading customs. He

armed some tribes, but not others. He dispensed firearms, bolts
of cloth, and quarts of "Indian Corn," but he also brought dis-
ease and starvation. The death of these Natives was, in his own
words, "an Unrecoverable Loss to ye Company." In their deaths
Knight mourned first a drop in Company profits. Years later, in
the horrifying seasons of 1716, as the Natives starved to death
all around him, he would write: "It requires a Great Deal of Care
in a Man to Govern & Manage these People Rightly ..." The sentence, meant as a compliment to himself, stands as a credo of
colonial racism, and one of the first expressions on record of the
white man's burden.

Following his return to England in 1700, James Knight was made
a member of the London "Committee." He was, by now, the
Company's undisputed expert on all matters pertaining to the
Bottom of the Baye. Remarkably, in 1711, at the age of seventy
(or thereabouts) he agreed to return to Hudson's Bay as governor. Ill health prevented him from taking on this assignment.
    Three years later, presumably in better health, James Knight
sailed once more for the Bay for the purpose of overseeing the
surrender of the forts that remained in French hands. Sailing
with him was his deputy governor, Henry Kelsey. This man had
undertaken one of the most astonishing explorations in North
American history when, in 1690, he journeyed as far west as
what today is called The Pas, Manitoba; a thousand-mile trek
that lasted three years and made him the first white man to
lay eyes on (and hunt) grizzlies and buffalo in the Canadian
West. The prologue to Kelsey's record of this journey is written
entirely in rhyming verse. For this almost unbelievable undertaking he was paid £30, making it, according to some historians,
the cheapest exploration in history. It is revealing of the frugal

nature of the Hudson's Bay Company that when Kelsey was twice captured and imprisoned by the French, his employers refused to pay him. A skilled Native linguist, he was described early on as "an active Lad delighting much in Indian company." He once dismissed a man for "beating and using all Indians Morosely." He is also on record as having done some trade in "sea horse teeth." Knight would eventually level complaints against Kelsey; the complaints are lost but are thought to have centred on the man being, in Knight's view, too generous and sympathetic to the Indians. The coolness that developed between these two men would soon play a part in one of the bleakest tragedies in the history of exploration.

In November of 1714 while at York Fort, Knight met a Chipewyan woman who had escaped from the Cree. She is known in history as "Thanadelthur," although for some reason in his diaries Knight referred to her only as "the slave woman." Over the next several years he would rely heavily on her as translator, guide, peacemaker, and torchbearer of his dreams of gold. In June of 1715 he sent "the slave woman," a contingent of Natives, and an officer, William Stuart, on a mission to further Company trade by promoting peace between the Cree and the northern Chipewyans. The expedition, it turned out, had another purpose. "Above all," Knight instructed Stuart, "you are to make a Strict Enquirry abt. there Mineralls ... if you find any Mineralls amongst them You must seem indifferent not letting them know ... it is of any value." He exhorted finally, "bring back some of Every sort you see."

In late April Knight received a grim note from Stuart indicating that the party had eaten their dogs and were subsisting on moss. Stuart himself had not eaten in eight days.

"Wee are in a Starving Condition at this time ... I do not think as I shall see you any more but I have a good heart." Despite these hardships Thanadelthur and the contingent returned a year later with some 160 of her countryman. Through her efforts a peace had been established. William Stuart never fully recovered from this expedition. Three years later Kelsey would write that Stuart had "been lunatick 3 or 4 times insomuch that wee have forct to tye him in his bed." He died insane at Fort York in 1719 at the age of 41. He had been employed by the Company since a boy of thirteen.

By 1715, circumstances had already began to turn against James Knight. Early in the year the spring breakup of the Hayes River occurred so swiftly that Knight and his men were forced to flee from the dinner table, leaving the fort severely damaged by ice. An incident occurred in the summer that precipitated the dreadful year to come, when Captain Joseph Davies brought a supply ship into the Bay, but mistook a signal fire for a star, and returned to England, without finding his way to York Fort.

By failing to supply trade goods for the Indians, some of who had come hundreds of miles, Joseph Davies ensured their destruction. Unable to receive shot and power or muskets, the Chipewyans were unwilling to return home against the heavily armed Upland Cree, who had not agreed to peace. In the winter that followed, some were taken into the fort for safety. Living on European rations and in close quarters with Europeans, they slowly began to die. Outside the palisades, their countrymen were starving. Knight wrote, "There was never more Indians came down ... than was that Summer ... but we had nothing for them; wch abundance of them Indians lost their lives ... by being starved ... There is near a 3rd part of the Indians in ye Country dead one way or another." Knight railed savagely against Joseph Davies for the rest of his life. The Company fired him and he remains on record in Canadian history as the man "remembered not for what he did, but for what he failed to do." Fortunately a supply ship arrived in September and a final and utter catastrophe was barely averted.

By December of 1716, Thanadelther lay in Fort York, having taken sick. It is here, in his concern for this remarkable Chipewyan woman, that James Knight reveals himself as something other than a heartless "Goldfinder." On February 5, 1717, when Thanadelther died after a long illness during which Knight personally attended her, he confided to his journal "I am almost ready to break my heart." He closed the day's entry noting the weather was finest, but the day was, "the most Melancholys't by the Loss of her." Here is the first sense of a vulnerable James Knight, almost pitiable in his grief. The more familiar portrait intrudes when he adds that her death "will be very Prejudiciall to the Company's Interest," and that he "gave a few odd things" to her countrymen "to wipe away their Sorrow."

By the winter of 1717, having watched the Natives starve, having seen Thanadelther die, Knight himself was taken sick and given to frequent fainting attacks. "For my part," he wrote, "I am weary of having the name of a Governor of this country ..." By September of 1718, the name was no longer his and Knight left for England; a harsh and arduous sailing that nearly killed him.. His tenure as governor was over. All that remained was his dreadful and terrifying end.

II

Marble Island lies twenty-five miles off the west coast of Hudson's Bay at what today is called Rankin Inlet. Approximately ten miles in length, it shines a brilliant white beneath open skies, and, according to legend, or at least one legend, owes its creation to an Inuit woman's urge to relieve herself. It is this innocuous detail which causes her to forfeit her life to a spirit in exchange for turning a clump of ice into land. The woman perishes while crawling on her hands and knees up the newly created earth. That land is today the shining quartzite of Marble Island and her death is the reason for an odd tradition: all those who land there for the first time must crawl up the shore on their hands and knees. Those who refuse are said to suffer terrible misfortune on the anniversary of their landing.

If anything can be said with certainty regarding the final days of James Knight and his doomed crews, it was that they were ignorant of this tradition. Arguably it was their ignorance of Inuit culture in general that accounts for what has been called the greatest mystery in Arctic exploration.

By March of 1719, having been back in England less than four months, James Knight was already in front of the Committee pressing them to outfit an expedition on a search for gold and copper. At first reluctant, the Committee agreed only after Knight threatened to circumvent them and seek outside financing. By June 4, Knight, outfitted with two ships, the *Albany* and *Discovery*, had received his sailing orders:

> You are with the first Opertunity of Wind and Weathr to Depart Gravesend on your Intended Voyages by God's Permission to find out the Streight of Annian [Northwest Passage] in Order to Discover Gold and Other Valuable Comodities to the Northward.

So confident was Knight of finding gold that he had on board with him specially constructed treasure chests bound in iron, to hold it. The two ships, carrying about thirty-five men between them, departed Gravesend harbour on June 4, 1719, and sailed west into utter oblivion.

The remnants of a massive stone building used to house his men, and a separate building for James Knight, are still visible on the eastern corner of Marble Island today. The *Albany* and *Discovery* lie in five fathoms of water, just off shore, although why the ships landed there remains a mystery. Bricks taken off the ships can still be found scattered about, as well as a circle of scoured earth; all that remains of some fifteen chaldrons of coal off-loaded to shore.

It has long been assumed that the *Albany* and *Discovery* were either damaged at sea or wrecked attempting to enter the harbour at Marble Island in the autumn of 1719. It follows that Knight, his two captains, and crew attempted to winter, ran short of supplies, and died one by one from a combination of cold, starvation, and scurvy. This interpretation was set in stone by Samuel Hearne who landed on the island in 1769 and interrogated several elderly Inuit. His recounting of how the ships were damaged entering the harbour and how "sickness and famine occasioned such havock among the English that by the setting in of the second Winter their number was reduced to twenty," established itself into the popular imagination.

According to Hearne's account, after the second winter, visiting "Esquimaux" returned to find only five Englishmen left alive. The sufferers were provided with seal flesh and whale blubber which "disordered them so much that 3 of them died in a few days and the other two, though very weak, made a shift to bury them." Reportedly these final two survivors made their way, daily, to a point of rock "and earnestly looked to the South and East as if in expectation of some vessels coming to their relief. At length one of the two died, and the other's strength was so far exhausted that he fell down and died also, in attempting to dig a grave for his companion."

This account, with its insistence on the role of the Christian burial service and the stern warning against those who stray and who at any moment must face God's wrath, is a grim one. Even at first glance there are problems with it. How exactly do thirty-five able-bodied British seamen land on an island and over the course of three years allow themselves to starve into extinction? These were far from incompetent men. Captain Berley, of the *Albany*, was obviously a quick-thinking individual. When the French marched to the front gate of Fort Albany in 1704 and demanded entrance, Berley, on watch at the time, answered that the governor was sleeping, but that he himself would get the key. Instead he opened two portholes and discharged two six-pound cannons into the enemy and completely routed the attack.

George Vaughan, who captained the *Discovery*, was also no novice. In 1714, while sailing the sloop *Eastmain* into Hudson's Bay, a sudden storm left the ship entirely sheathed in ice and on the verge of foundering. Vaughan was part of a crew that coolly sailed her directly into the rocky shore and saved themselves. "You cannot have a soberer or brisker man," concluded James Knight. With these two in charge of the ships, and Knight as commander in chief, the expedition that left Gravesend on June 4 was arguably the most experienced to ever enter Hudson's Bay.

Perhaps the largest hole in the Hearne account is the absence of graves. Typically, Hudson's Bay Company employees were buried formally with the rites of the English church. Yet the graves are not there. The Beattie and Geiger examination conducted over four years in the late 1980s and early 1990s revealed very few traces of human bones and nothing remotely resembling a graveyard, as indicated from the Hearne story. There is simply no evidence of the orderly burying of men as they succumbed one by one to starvation, frostbite, and scurvy. Just as telling was a diver's examination of the foundered ships, which indicated they were not damaged at all, but had made harbour safely. The successful offloading of materials, including a prefabricated house for Knight, 3,500 bricks, and a massive amount of coal, indicates a well-equipped crew preparing in an orderly fashion to survive a harsh winter.

Exactly what went wrong remains unknown, although there is evidence that the ultimate cause of the tragedy lay in a combination of petty intrigues and an appalling and eventually fatal ignorance of the "Eskemays." Despite the competence of his men, despite his own vast experience, the Knight expedition, with the exception of Vaughan, who had brief contact a year earlier, was entirely ignorant of the Inuit. All Knight knew of the "Eskemays" came from the Cree, traditional enemies who viewed the northerners with terror. Knight knew little more than the commonplace fabulation that they drank their victims' blood "the way an Englishman drinks his ale." Perhaps the most fatal shortcoming would involve the inevitable and total ignorance of the language.

Given this background, it is possible to formulate another scenario of what happened out there on that shining island. It involves two civilizations making contact, moving cautiously toward each other on a wind-smoothed surface of quartzite. One knows nothing about the other. Under these circumstances the inevitable happens, something goes wrong: somehow a false move is made, an item stolen, perhaps a musket discharged, voices get raised, a few men surge forward. Accusations are levelled, but not understood, amends are offered, words of appeasement, again, tragically, not understood. An Inuk points his finger, a British sailor panics, slashes out with a sabre, leaving the "green" scar, the visible proof of European presence carved onto the very face of another civilization. A fight erupts, then breaks off. The Inuit retreat to the western rim of the island, the English remain established in the east. A standoff has been reached. The diplomacy, the tact, the language required to resolve this conflict is entirely lacking. Knight, assumed to be perhaps eighty years old, was not like Kelsey, "a man who delighted much in Indian company." His own proud and testy nature would itself work against a peaceful resolution. The English, he reasoned, were well-armed. They could look after themselves. What need did they have of the "Eskemay?" In the end the need was absolute; in particular the need to comprehend Inuit diet.

The relationship between fresh meat and scurvy was only dimly understood in Knight's time, and Knight probably understood it as well as anyone. His expedition had packed out enough meat to last a winter. Enormous quantities of salt taken on board indicate the men expected to find fresh game thereafter. Knight had a great deal of experience with fresh game. He knew the deer and moose, the partridge, the goose. Conceivably, he expected to find these creatures north of latitude 64. He did not. Instead he found walrus, seal, and whale. Tellingly, Knight is on record to the effect that an Englishman is not a dog; he does not eat his meat raw. This inability to fathom the ways of the Inuit, the unadaptable clinging to British habits, would have killing effects. Over the winter the supplies of packed meat would run out; the island's few hares could not support thirty-five men for long. Even the ability to hunt may have been restricted by the Inuit. The very people whose guidance and intelligence was so desperately required were now enemies, encamped on the other side of the island. Slowly at first, then quickly, the debilitating effects of scurvy would make themselves felt. The teeth loosen and drop, bleeding begins beneath the skin, the cartilage degenerates until a man is unable to even lift himself from the ground. Under these circumstances the English muskets would count for nothing. Ironically, and terribly, James Knight and his men, surrounded by animals whose flesh is filled with ascorbic acid, may have perished because of the absence of it in their own diets.

During the time that Knight and his men were mysteriously perishing on Marble Island, Henry Kelsey sent a ship north of Churchill. Its captain, John Hancock, returned in September of 1720 with news that the "Goldfinders," as Kelsey termed them, had met with the "Eskemays" and "spoilt our trade." The remark is problematic. Does it mean the Inuit were flush with goods supplied by Knight's men and required no further trade? Or does it mean they had become so angered with the men on Marble Island that they would have nothing to do with English traders? Either way the remark reveals the sort of trouble that James Knight was capable arousing.

The tensions that existed between Knight and Kelsey were significant. Kelsey, who had succeeded Knight as governor of the Baye, was the one man empowered to undertake a rescue. In April 1721, with Englishmen conceivably still alive on Marble Island, Kelsey sailed north up the west coast of Hudson's Bay and then turned back, noting casually in his journal, "I bore away because ye winds did not favour my intentions ..." The friction between these two men was so obvious that Company officials ordered the expedition's captains not to sail south of latitude 64, except under "Utmost Extremity Only to preserve Shipps Sloop & Men's lives." The area south of 64 was the jurisdiction of Henry Kelsey. Knight himself was under orders that should he encounter Kelsey or any of his men, to show them "all Possible Respect and neither Molest or Hinder them ..."

By 1721, articles from the Knight expedition began ominously showing up in the possession of Inuit and the Natives they traded with. Kelsey's failure to launch a rescue operation the following year is equally unconscionable and likely based on malice alone. The allegations that Knight brought against him were in Kelsey's term "odious," undermining a reputation which he considered "more Valuable yn Life itselfe."

It is possible the truth or at least one of the truths of the Knight expedition was to be found in accounts of a lost journal belonging to Hudson's Bay Company employee Master John Scroggs. The interpretation of Scroggs as a timid, incompetent navigator has tended to cast doubt on the man's findings. Nonetheless it is reported in July of 1722 by Richard Staunton, Hudson's Bay Company factor at Churchill, that Scroggs "doth Affirm that Every Man was Killed by the Eskemoes wch I am heartily sorry for their hard fortune." Scroggs also reported seeing in the Marble Island area an Inuk man with "a large Scar on his Cheek, like a Cut with a Cutless, and at that time a Green Wound." There being no other Europeans in this area but the Knight expedition, the observation is telling and chilling.

In 1724, the Hudson's Bay Company quietly closed the books on the doomed expedition. The *Albany* and *Discovery* were written off as complete losses. No rescue attempt or investigation was launched. Joseph Robson, a staunch critic of the Hudson's Bay Company, would soon suggest that "the company did not value the loss of ship and sloop" as long as James Knight was gotten rid of. Knight's will was executed in 1724. It contains further proof of the man; he bequeaths his son "one shilling and no more he having been already advanced by me in the world Considerably more than my Circumstances could allow of."

It is this sort of spite and vanity that James Knight put forth and the same spite and vanity that he received in return. Even the massive mound of coal unloaded by Knight's men was not immune to it. Ransacked over the years by visiting whalers, it was finally set on fire by an American captain for no reason but to spite the British and prevent them from using it. The scoured ring is still visible. The morbid fascination of Marble Island with its Inuit and whalers' graves, its ghosts, its bloody history, its legends, and its blistering winds, lives on. There are Inuit today who will not land there.

As for Knight's dreams of mineral wealth, they unfolded at last into the North Rankin Nickel Mine established in the 1950s. Situated on the mainland west of Marble Island, it was built to meet the nickel demands created by the Korean War, and closed unceremoniously a few years later. Today the rusted remains of a massive concentrator dominate the skyline; the last visible reminder of a man and his tragic search for riches.

2

Savage Soil:
The Life and Death of John Richardson

"Canada was not generous to her first novelist."
— William Riddell, 1923

At the age of fifteen, he shook Tecumseh's hand only hours before the great Shawnee leader was killed in battle. By sixteen he was a veteran of five military campaigns. A year later he was a prisoner of war. At nineteen he sailed to Europe and fought his first duel. The next year found him in uniform in the Barbados, where he saw the heads of slaves mounted on poles. At the age of twenty-two, he was gambling in the salons of Paris and fighting more duels, many more duels. He went to Spain and fought in the Carlist wars where in one battle he was shot three times. He married, separated, remarried, and was widowed. In middle age he moved from Canada to New York City, where he lived and died in appalling poverty. In the meantime he did something no English-speaking Canadian had ever done before — he wrote books. His name was John Richardson.

* * *

He was born was born October 4, 1796, probably in today's Niagara-on-the-Lake. His grandfather, the fur trader John Askin, personally owned 7 million acres of North American land, all of which he surrendered rather than pledge an oath of allegiance to the United States. His grandmother was a Native woman, possibly Ottawa, and his father Robert, a Scottish surgeon, spent a portion of his career inoculating Natives against smallpox. His mother, Madeline, was cultured, bilingual, and educated in the Convent de Notre Dame in Montreal. She would die of tuberculosis when her son was thirteen.

John Richardon's early years were passed in Detroit, where he was cared for by his Askin grandparents. Later, reunited with his family in Amherstburg, Canada, he began schooling, which he despised, and where in his own words he was "more frequently flogged than the greatest dunce." In 1812, the Americans declared war, and, to Richardson's joy, schools were shut down. "I felt disposed to bless the Americans," he wrote.

He at once enlisted as a fifteen-year-old gentleman officer and marched to war. In his first exposures to the battlefield he saw "the pestilential exhalations arising from the naked and putrid bodies of horses and men." By sixteen he had seen scalps and other parts of human skin drying in the sun. The skin, he noted coolly, was, "principally taken from the hands and feet." Richardson fought alongside Native forces at Moraviantown, under the command of Tecumseh, the great leader who spread a doomed message of tribal unification against European encroachment. Earlier in the day, Tecumseh had walked the British line, shaking hands with every officer in it, including the young and deeply impressed Richardson. Hours later he was killed in action, his body mutilated by American soldiers. Richardson, taken prisoner, was marched inland in the rain, ending up in a prisoner of war camp in Frankfort, Kentucky.

As an officer he received preferential treatment and was allowed to socialize at the home of an American woman. There, during tea, he directed a cutting remark to a young American officer who lit up a cigar in front of several disapproving young ladies. The enraged youth tried to murder Richardson with a stiletto, but failed when the Canadian knocked down a gate and escaped.

In the fall of 1814, he was back on Canadian soil and shipped to Kingston, where for five months he lay in his barracks, wracked by fever. In the spring he embarked for Quebec City aboard the first steamship to ply the St. Lawrence River, then sailed to England and was keenly disappointed to learn that Napoleon had been defeated at Waterloo, leaving him no one to fight.

One afternoon, leaving a London theatre, he overheard a young man criticize the acting of a nineteen-year-old girl and challenged him to a duel. The actress, Eliza Vestris, was famous for her legs, which would soon be cast in plaster by an Italian sculptor. "Such a leg," stated the sculptor, "was always certain to fetch a high price." Richardson's first duel was fought in Hyde Park without injury to either party.

A short time later he shipped to the Barbados, an appointment that came his way thanks to the efforts of John Norton, a friend of the Askin family. Norton, the child of a Cherokee mother and Scottish father, would translate the Gospel of St. Mark and perhaps even Walter Scott's *The Lady of the Lake* into Mohawk. In middle age he married a sixteen-year-old Native girl and later, in Canada on the Six Nations reserve near Brantford, shot dead the young man he presumed to be her lover. Convicted and fined a hundred pounds, he undertook a guilt-ridden journey into the American South and was never seen again.

Richardson arrived in Barbados on the winter of 1816. While crossing the equator, the ship's crew tried to initiate him by shaving his head, a prank played on all first-time voyagers, but one that the young man found irksome — Richardson drew a pistol and threatened to kill anyone who came near him. Once on the island, Richardson's colleagues began to die immediately of yellow fever. During his short stay he saw the heads of rebellious slaves rotting on poles, learned of the summary execution of a thousand black men in revenge for the death of two white slave owners, and was appalled by the sexual liaisons imposed on slave girls as young as twelve. Later, thinking back on this time, Richardson would ask, "Is cruelty then, inseparable from power?"

At the age of twenty-two, John Richardson, now dark and handsome, was back on the Continent, where he moved easily with the Regency demimonde of the twenties. He took up gambling, in particular *écarté*, at which he became skilled. By 1821 he was living in Paris, a much cheaper base of operations for an officer on half pay. He may have spent time there in a debtor's prison, but if so was out in time to duel the Marquis du Hally, who had already killed at least two English officers. Richardson took a ball in the heel.

When not duelling, he ran with a crowd of young poets, gamblers, and a preposterously rich Englishman who sent a servant in front of him to collect the names and addresses of pretty women he spotted on the street. There was even Nicholas Bochsa, a celebrated harpist and wanted forger. He also found time to marry and began, perhaps through his wife's connections, to publish. In 1825, *The New Monthly Magazine* printed the first installment of his 1812 war narrative, *A Canadian Campaign*. He followed this with the long poem "Tecumseh, or the Warrior of the West in four cantos with notes," of which a critic at the time wrote "the feeling that prompted it is better than the execution." The poem contains several lines predicting the haunted relationship Richardson would carry on with the land of his birth:

> Still there are those who ...
> Fain renew upon that savage soil
> Their first privations

Then came *Écarté*, probably the first English-language novel to be written by anyone born in Canada. With this book, Richardson also became the first Canadian writer to be smeared by a critic. William Jerden, believing Richardson to be another Richardson to whom he was hostile, wrote that *Écarté* could not be described without "polluting our paper," and was "unfit to be seen beyond the ... stews" — meaning the sewers of London. Remarkably, Richardson refrained from shooting the man even though the review killed sales of the book in England and led to the author getting dropped by his publisher. A pirated edition, for which he received nothing, sold better in the United States. Telling of these Byronic times, and perhaps more telling of Richardson himself, in *Écarté*, a woman spurned by her lover experiences emotions of such power that a blood vessel explodes in her head and she dies.

In 1830 he published the poem "Kensington Gardens in 1830," an indiscreet "satirical trifle by the author of Ecarte." With this early work Richardson turned the tables on a literary form that was already centuries old: the European who comes to the New World and writes about it for readers back home. Richardson, born and raised in the hardwood forests of southern Ontario, was in Europe, writing books about the foibles of Europeans. Two years later he published the novel that is widely regarded as the beginning of Canadian literature.

Wacousta, or the Prophecy, a Tale of the Canadas has remained in print almost continuously for nearly a century and a half. It has been required reading in a number of university Canadian literature courses, was turned into a play by James Reaney in the 1970s, and proved central to Northrop Frye's influential theory of "the garrison mentality." The heroine in Marian Engel's 1976 novel *Bear* falls asleep clutching a copy of it. Today the novel can be purchased, or at least ordered, from any bookstore in the country or online retailer.

Wacousta is a story dominated by a scream. Throughout its more than five hundred dense pages, men act with incredible bravery, but to no avail, and die brutally at the hands of a murderer. Their "oozing brains" are licked off the earth by "wolf-dogs." Children are scalped, a woman is taunted before she is raped and murdered. A man successfully disguises himself as a beaver. Infuriating lapses in logic cause an innocent man to be charged, convicted, and instantly executed. A women pronounces a terrible curse over the corpse of her husband. Bodies fall from the sky and land on the decks of ships. Men who open their mouths to speak are frequently dead before their sentence is finished. A dense and extraordinarily claustrophobic novel, *Wacousta* contains some 175,000 words, and, at times it seems, an equal number of characters. A man named De Haldimar must not be confused with a man named de Haldimar. In the grand Gothic tradition, bosoms heave, blood curdles, and on two occasions "the vampire of despair banquets on [people's] hearts."

Wacousta is also a template for Canadian literary racism. Despite his own probable if distant Native origins, his admiration for Tecumseh and Native life, Richardson wrote for the white audience of his times: "Injins" are lumped together as a nameless seething treacherous mass who scalp people, shriek, and sling beautiful blond-haired women across their shoulders. Wacousta himself is a white man. The subtleties and complexities of Native languages are reduced to the single word, "Uggh."

The book is also strangely brilliant: a barely respectable literary uniqueness, stained with madness and violence and situated on the edges of a startling eroticism:

> The female...fixed her dark and brilliant eyes upon the tall and picturesque form of the rifleman whose active and athletic limbs, thrown into powerful relief by the distension of each nerve and muscle, appeared to engross her whole admiration and interest ...

This astonishing passage is not something the reader will ever find in the novels of Jane Austen or, arguably, in the novels of anyone else then writing. In Richardson's work both the male and female body are constantly being gazed at and lusted over. The sexual urge would become even more visible in his future work, especially the late novels *Westbrook* and the scandalous if not pornographic *The Monk Knight of St. John*.

As soon as *Wacousta* rolled off the press, Richardson sent a signed copy to the King of England, and followed that up with a letter. His Majesty's secretary wrote back and assured the eager young author that *Wacousta* was inspiring "deep interest," and had "been read by the whole Court."

In 1835, Richardson left for Spain as part of a mercenary British force fighting the Carlist rebels, a coalition of Basques who opposed the rule of the Spanish Queen. He took his new wife with him, Maria Drayson — what happened to Richardson's first wife is not known. In Spain he quickly got on the wrong side of his commanding officers, most of whom were cruel and incompetent in Richardson's mind. He received a promotion, was denied another, fell sick with typhoid and was unconscious for nine days. At some point his commander demanded to read Richardson's journal, believing (correctly) that it might be critical of himself. After further intrigues Richardson was transferred, made captain of the 6th Scotch Regiment and participated in the bloody battle of St. Bartholomew, where he was shot in the chest and twice in the arms. After taking his third shot, he was advised by the surgeon to leave the battlefield and, as a result, was soon facing a court martial for "cowardice in battle." After successfully defending himself he wrote and published a lengthy attack on his former commander.

In the spring of 1837 Richardson and his wife Maria embarked on the SS *Ontario* bound for Canada via New York. Richardson had convinced the conservative newspaper *The Times* to hire him to report on the troubles in the Canadas. It was *The Times'* assumption that Richardson shared their contempt for reform, which probably he did; Richardson's twenty-one-year-old brother had been part of the gang that forced their way into William Lyon Mackenzie's house, vandalized his printing press, and heaved the type into Lake Ontario. In one of Richardson's first dispatches he ridiculed Mackenzie and "his mad and impotent career of treason." But in Montreal he became fast friends and a great admirer of Lord Durham, who was being vilified back in England in *Times* editorials. Richardson wrote glowingly of Durham's effort and was fired for his views.

Undaunted, Richardson contributed political articles to newspapers, edited Canadian journals, shopped his *Personal Memoirs* to publishers, acquired a dog named Hector, and established himself as a one-man Canadian literary industry. He also continued to make powerful enemies, was challenged to a duel by a man he did not consider worthy of duelling, and later found the lampposts of Montreal covered with posters proclaiming Richardson to be a coward. He then agreed to the duel but could find no one to act as a second. The duel was cancelled and he was again postered as a coward. In a cruel slight both he and his wife were refused admission to the regimental ball and dance. Ostracized, he and Maria left Montreal, departing in May 1839 along with their dog Hector, journeying across Canada to a rented home in what is now Windsor. Here Richardson finished *The Canadian Brothers, or the Prophecy Fulfilled*, a sequel to *Wacousta*. Unknown as a novelist in his native country, he was something of a celebrity in Detroit, where *Wacousta*, in a pirated edition, had been avidly read and successfully staged. Trouble continued to follow him — an advertisement appeared in a Vermont newspaper and was republished in Detroit, urging that he be shot on sight as a British spy.

By November he was back in Montreal arranging for the publication of *The Canadian Brothers*. The subscription lists were disappointingly small and Richardson penned one of the first known rebukes of the reading habits of Canadians: "The people here are too much of pounds, shilling and pence men to care much about polite literature … they would far more rejoice in a grand distiller of whiskey than a writer of books."

After arranging for the publication of his book, he bought a sleigh and two horses, loaded the sleigh with copies of his new novel and set out in January in an effort, in reverse, to match or better the record recently set by Governor General Charles Poulett Thompson — Toronto to Montreal, 360 miles in thirty-six hours. Everything went wrong; Richardson reinjured his wounded arm in a tumble, the road turned to mud and he was forced to walk beside the sleigh for sixty-five miles. After many stops, he reached Windsor, was challenged to a duel by the estranged husband of his first cousin, only to have the duel interrupted by a justice of the peace who reminded Richardson that duelling was against

Canadian law. Richardson insisted he was just out duck hunting
(with pistols) perhaps consciously echoing the strange scene in
Wacousta where two British officers negotiate a perilous journey
by disguising themselves as duck hunters.

In June of 1841 Richardson and Maria moved to a cottage in
Brockville, where Richardson sold his military commission to
buy a printing press. In Brockville he was embroiled in further
conflicts, one of which saw him writing a pamphlet to attack an
opponent, followed up by the suggestion they meet to exchange
pistol shots at five paces. This affair only further damaged
Richardson's spotty reputation. He then began publication of
The New Era, or the Canadian Chronicle, with the stated intent
of introducing real literature (his own) to Canada. He raised
few subscribers, although he did manage, in his garden, to raise
watermelons, perhaps the first Canadian to succeed at this.

By 1841 he had petitioned Lord Sydenham to create a
fund to support destitute artists, but was denied. In the fester-
ing Canadas of the 1840s, his enemies grew more numerous,
blocking any sort of appointment he might receive. His dog,
Hector, was poisoned. Richardson is said to have wept over this
and posted a reward for the killers. In recompense he tamed a
deer and kept it as a pet. His cottage was reclaimed and children taunted him in public — so much so that Richardson took
to rebuking them in his newspaper. His book *The War of 1812*,
which he had reason to believe would replace the American
texts being taught in Canadian schools, was ignored. Putting
his printing press in hock, Richardson, Maria, and the deer,
moved to Kingston, where he received £250 from the government to continue his historical writings on the 1812 conflict.
In 1843, he got his press back and began publishing his second

newspaper, *The Canadian Loyalist and Spirit of 1812*. The paper was lively and well-read with Richardson, as usual, contributing most of the copy, and still displaying, even in a theatre review, his singular scrutiny on female beauty and the human form: "As Mrs. Chatterly in *The Widow's Victim*, she looked and acted like a blooming girl of 18 — full of life, fun and frolic, and yet Mrs. Noah, we should say, has arrived at the full, ripe luxuriance of meridian womanhood."

The paper shut down for financial reasons at the end of 1844. By this time Richardson was campaigning for John A. Macdonald. Through the influence of his friend Lord Metcalf, he was appointed as superintendent of police for the Welland Canal works. With this appointment, Richardson incurred an enormous amount of resentment. Canal labourers worked in near slave conditions, earning two shillings a day for fifteen hours of back-breaking labour. When they attempted to strike, soldiers were called in and strikers were shot. Richardson entered the fray, despised by reformers, trusted by no one, and harassed daily in a series of petty and intrigues that saw him arrested on charges that included "walking violently," for which, in front of his wife, he was forcibly removed from his home and fined a shilling. In the face of this harassment, Maria fell ill. Richardson, forced to defend himself in court, was often away from the house. On August 16, 1845, at the age of thirty-seven, Maria Drayson Richardson died of apoplexy, while her husband rode desperately from the courthouse to be with her.

Richardson was left, in his own words, "desolate and without hope." For six months he did not enter a private house. In the evenings he worked on his manuscript, *Eight Years in Canada*. This book, unknown, and almost impossible to find, has been called "the main social commentary on the Canada of that day." In the face of mounting intrigue, Richardson's police force was disbanded. Richardson, unemployed, in debt, and friendless, stole away from St. Catharines in the middle of the night.

In Montreal, he started another newspaper called *the Weekly Expositor or Reformer of Public Abuses and Railway and Mining Intelligencer*, described by the Toronto *Globe* as "delightful" and "characterized by that … 'Whose dog are you?' sort of air.'" No copy of this newspaper has ever been found. At some point he wrote a letter to the district clerk at Niagara who was hounding him for his debts, and accused the "false government" of being instrumental in his wife's death, assuring them of his "unmixed detestation."

It was in this mood that he wrote and finished *The Monk Knight of St. John*, which to some scholars is just page after page of "lip-licking dirtiness." He also wrote a sequel to *Eight Years in Canada*, and predicted the end of the world in a letter titled "A Believer in Impending Doom to the Whole of the Present Human Race." When a young poet ridiculed Richardson's letter, Richardson challenged him to a duel, was brought to court, and ordered to keep the peace. Around this time his brother Charles, aged forty-two, died of alcoholism. Richardson travelled west to Windsor with his old Regency drinking buddy, the harpist Nicholas Boscha, and wrote a letter to Prime Minister Baldwin reminding him that he owed him five shillings for a copy of one of his books. Richardson apologizes for requesting such a trifle, but reminds the prime minister that he does not have the "advantage … of an office, fat or lean, under the Government." He went to Walpole Island and wrote about the beauty of the First Nations women that he saw there. He returned to Montreal and worked on two more novels, *Hardscrabble* and *Wau-nangee or the Massacre at Chicago*. While he worked, Canada's Parliament buildings were set on fire. Effigies burned in Toronto, and citizens hurled rocks at the governor general.

* * *

It is believed that John Richardson left for New York in May of 1849. His time was running out and perhaps he sensed it — his own letter predicting the end of the world slated the event for 1852.

At first things seemed to go well for the Canadian literary lion in New York. *Hardscrabble* and *Wau-nan-gee* were published immediately and to acclaim. Even the lurid *The Monk Knight of St. John* was printed, although the publisher thought it prudent to remove the company's name from the book. Two different stage versions of *Wacousta* were being performed in American cities. Richardson, irrepressibly, began to write songs, several of which received considerable attention. He was asked to give a lecture by the New York Historical Society. His stories appeared in American magazines, including an essay in which he denies the Native tribes of North America arrived from a "foreign source," but were, in fact, here on the continent "from the first creation."

For all of this he was going deeply and fatally broke. "Will you lend me ten to fifteen dollars," he wrote to an American acquaintance, Rufus Griswold, who would eventually become literary executor to another tough-luck writer — Edgar Allan Poe. Richardson was selling his books for next to nothing, gladly changing the content of what he had envisioned as a Canadian national literature to fit into an American context. Richardson no longer had any illusions about creating a Canadian identity. Of his own books he said, "they might as well have been written in Kamchatka as Canada." He also wrote the novel *Westbrook*, a monstrously cruel work about a rapist. That Richardson even wrote this book was not established until 1972, when a copy of the novel was found printed in an old New York newspaper. In yet another doomed literary adventure, he penned a book in defence of a Bavarian prostitute, Lola Montes, who was on her way to New York, and being savagely attacked by the American press. Richardson, in a quixotic and knightly gesture, paid for the publication himself and plodded from one bookseller to another in a fruitless effort to sell the book. He may well have attempted to court Lola Montes, as well, but she ignored him and later suffered the indignity of getting herself tossed out of a Washington Square rooming house. The Bavarian prostitute would rebound from her troubles, but Richardson would not.

On May 12, 1852, Major John Richardson, author of *Wacousta*, and as many as six other books, starved to death on the street. In a story one hopes is apocryphal, he was last seen trying to sell his dog to a little girl in an attempt to buy food. The dog's name was again Hector, a reminder of days when Richardson, in his fighting prime, rambled the paths of Canada and Europe, entertaining the woman he loved with stories of his large and vigorous life. But that woman was dead and Richardson was very much alone. Apparently his final words were addressed to his dog. "Ah my poor Hector, we must part or starve." *The Pick*, which published his obituary, concluded simply, "such is the fate of genius." According to records at the time, the body of Canada's first novelist was taken from the city limits and buried in an undisclosed space. The grave has never been found.

"I certainly have no particular ambition to rank among [Canada's] future 'men of genius,'" he once wrote, "or to share in any posthumous honor they may be disposed to confer."

One suspects, or hopes that this is the just the bitter musings of a proud and neglected artist and that today, a century and a half after his appalling death, John Richardson would not object too strenuously if a few words were spoken in his favour.

3

The Duellists

The first recorded duel in Upper Canada took place in a frozen grove on January 3, 1800, at what is now the corner of Front and Berkeley Streets in downtown Toronto. At that spot, in the mud behind the government buildings, John White, the province's first attorney general, took a pistol shot above the right hip and died thirty-six hours later in excruciating pain.

By all accounts a diligent attorney general, White was also irascible and possessed a big mouth; in 1799 he found it necessary to apply to the Court of King's bench for protection against a captain of the Queen's Rangers, who wanted to shoot him. By January his loose lips had landed him in more trouble, this time for speaking "slightingly" of the wife of Major John Small, an Englishman arrived in Upper Canada to serve as clerk of the Executive Council. White had engaged in a brief affair with the man's wife, and, in a letter, had the ill grace to question her morals and even the legality of her marriage. When the attorney general failed to withdraw his "imputations," Major John Small challenged him to a duel.

By the law of England duelling was a criminal offence. A charge of murder was levelled against Major Small and he was brought before Judge Henry Allcock, a vindictive man given to "paroxysms of Madness" who insisted on the full pomp of the English court even though he presided over a jurisdiction of mud and mosquitoes. Three years later at the assizes at Windsor (then called Sandwich), Allcock would sentence a man and woman to be hanged until dead and then hanged again, in chains. To Allcock's chagrin, the jury acquitted Small.

John White, Upper Canada's first known victim of a fatal duel, died heavily in debt, unable to make provisions for his mistress and the two daughters he fathered by her. He was buried in his own garden near Sherbourne and Bloor Streets, and, seventy-one years later, suffered the indignity of having his bones dug up by a gang of labourers shovelling for building sand.

The man who shot him lived for another thirty-two years. His signature, "John Small, C.E.C." can be found on most of the correspondence originating from the offices that controlled Upper Canada. Following the duel, his wife was ostracized by the elite of Toronto, who entertained few doubts as to her morals, and refused to even talk to her for some eight years. Her husband's promotion to the Legislative Council was postponed indefinitely, and he would have died a pauper if not for some lucky real-estate speculation. Trounced in an 1801 by-election, he suffered the humiliation of having only two friends vote for him. The victor in that election, Angus Macdonell, perished three years later when His Majesty's Vessel, *Speedy*, sank in Lake Ontario, taking with it five percent of York's entire population of four hundred.

As to the frozen patch of mud where Mrs. Small's honour was vindicated, and where John White was fatally wounded, it is now a car wash.

II

The province's next fatal duel occurred less than a mile away. In 1817, it was the site of a barn that belonged to Chief Justice Elmsley. One of Upper Canada's more whimsical letter writers, he wrote to a friend: "There is no news here except the death of my Parrot who departed this life the day before yesterday without a will." It was near his barn the young sons of two prominent families exchanged shots, one of which ended the life of John Ridout, age eighteen.

The origins of the duel lay in an obscure family resentment that had simmered for two years. According to Mr. Justice Riddell, who took an interest in these matters some ninety years later, Samuel Jarvis left York in 1815 to place his youngest sister in a Quebec boarding school. Travelling with them, under his protection, was Miss Ridout, who was to be boarded at the same school. What followed was a complicated glut of brothers, sisters, meddling mothers, wayward letters, and the desire of a backwater aristocracy to keep its fragile dignity intact.

Perhaps the sight of Mississauga Indians pitching wigwams on Yonge Street had something to do with the fragility of that dignity. But the original slight itself can hardly be ascertained even by the sharp legal eyes of Mr. Justice Riddell. Apparently Miss Jarvis was to have her accounts paid by Thomas Ridout, who was then to be reimbursed by Samuel Jarvis. A year later, Mrs. Ridout entered the fray, somehow became convinced her son had been obliged to support the girl without reimbursement, and chattered this information throughout the insular world of the Family Compact.

The result was a letter from Samuel Jarvis to Mr. Ridout Sr. (surveyor general of Upper Canada), who then passed the letter on to his son George (later treasurer of the Law Society) who then wrote back to Jarvis, who then demanded an apology with the option of "meeting me with your friend Saturday morning next seven o'clock at the Five Mile Meadow opposite Brown's Point."

The duel was accepted and called off because of scheduling problems. Later rescheduled, it was prevented a second time by the intervention of famous educator Reverend John Strachan. Strachan, a friend of both families, had arrived in Upper Canada in 1813 and found the local government to be "composed of ignorant clowns." He had the habit of wearing his left boot on his right foot, and vice versa, in an attempt to make his boots last longer. When American Forces took York for a second time, he managed, in a remarkable piece of diplomacy, to convince the United States Commodore Isaac Chauncy to return some books that his soldiers had looted in the first invasion. A colleague later called him the most spiteful man in Upper Canada.

Despite the intervention of the teacher, the Jarvis and Ridout clans maintained their animosity. "They do everything in their power to crush our house," wrote a biblical Thomas Ridout. In 1817, his young brother John was conducting a lawsuit against the father of Samuel Jarvis and managed to get himself thrown out of Jarvis's office. Several days later, the two young men met on the street. There in the mud, witnessed by a few sagging pines, the sons of two of Upper Canada's prominent families went at it. Ridout reportedly shattered a few bones in Jarvis's hand before the combatants were separated by a war hero named FitzGibbon, and his companion, Dr. Robert Horne, who later had his house burned down, personally, by William Lyon Mackenzie. Late in life, Horne dedicated himself to a essay on the subject of "nuisances," particularly soapsuds that "accumulate in pools ... and become exceedingly offensive."

A challenge was carried to Jarvis two days after this dustup on behalf of John Ridout. The challenge was accepted and at daylight on July 12, the two young men and their seconds assembled close to what is now the corner of College and Yonge.

It is not clear what John Ridout or Samuel Peters Jarvis knew about duelling. No doubt they, or their seconds, were aware of the Code Duello, adopted at the Clonmel Summer Assizes in 1777; a manual put together by the gentleman of the Irish counties, and containing the twenty-six commandments of duelling. Unfortunately, the friends, or "seconds," paid no attention to Commandment XX, which states: "Seconds are bound to attempt a reconciliation before the meeting takes place." Nor would anyone gathered outside of Elmsley's barn be privy to the remark made decades later by a sophisticated French duellist: "it is not swords or pistols that kill, but seconds …" In this case the choice of seconds indicates how compact the Family Compact was: Ridout's second was James Small, son of the man who had shot dead the attorney general sixteen years earlier. Representing Jarvis was a young Mr. Henry John Boulton, who, at the trial, would force the attorney general to remove himself from the case: Boulton was his son.

At daybreak, on July 12, the two young antagonists and their seconds met and retired into Elmsley's barn, waiting for a rain to pass. (The French critic Sainte-Beuve later circumvented this problem by showing up for a duel with an umbrella in one hand, pistol in the other, "I don't mind being killed," he said, "but I'll be damned if I'm going to catch a cold.")

The principals were placed sixteen yards apart and both parties agreed on a signal of "one, two, three, fire!" James Small had just pronounced "two" when Ridout either out of calumny, nerves, or bad luck, raised his arm and discharged his pistol (Jarvis would later insist it was a deliberate attempt to murder him). Regardless, both seconds acted in accordance with Commandment XIX of the Code Duello: "In all cases a misfire is equivalent to a shot." Ridout was instructed to stand back in. "I will," he said, "but give me another pistol." The seconds conferred, gave Ridout another pistol, then took it back on the grounds that "Jarvis was entitled to his shot."

Three years earlier, John Ridout had fought the Americans on Lake Ontario as a midshipman in the provincial navy. He was now eighteen year old and stood unarmed before his opponent. At the call of "one, two, three, fire!" Samuel Jarvis raised his pistol and fired. Ridout slumped. Jarvis cried out, "My God, what have I done!" The duellists then shook hands and apologized.

"I forgive you," said Ridout. According to a contemporary account "the three then fled to town leaving the dear youth alone in the agonies of death, vomiting up blood."

The duel enraged the citizenry of York, who viewed it as a cold-blooded murder. It also left in its wake a slab of limestone that can be seen today, cemented to the exterior lobby of St. James' Cathedral on King Street. This stone document stands next to a fragment from the original St. James's Church in Piccadilly, knocked loose by German bombers over London in 1940. Carved in the elegant lettering of the nineteenth century, it reads: "His filial affection, engaging manners, and nobleness of mind gave early promise of future excellence. This promise he gallantly fulfilled … At the return of Peace he commenced with ardour the study of the law and with fairest prospects; but a Blight came, and he was consigned to an early grave."

That blight was Samuel Peters Jarvis and the text shows the rage of Ridout's grieving mother, whose accusations started the whole mess two years earlier. For years afterward, she is said to have stood on the steps of St. James' Cathedral waiting for Jarvis's second, James Boulton, to exit, and would then curse him publicly for the murder of her son.

Samuel Peters Jarvis was acquitted, proving again the reluctance of Canadian juries to pass judgment on the outcome of a duel. Ten years later, enraged by being described in print as a murderer, Samuel Jarvis led the mob that heaved William Lyon Mackenzie's typescript into Lake Ontario. For this he was rewarded with an Indian commissionership, and later became a well-known defaulter on loans. In 1842, a three-man panel concluded Jarvis was incompetent and possibly dishonest, finding that £9,000 intended for Indian use had gone missing. It is possible that Jarvis had merely been defeated by the growing complexity of nineteenth-century bookkeeping. However, the tribunal looked dimly on reports that agents in his employ had bartered government goods to Indians in exchange for sexual favours. He died in 1856, leaving a Toronto street named after him.

III

The province's last-known fatal duel took place in the back-townships near the village of Perth, Ontario. It began with a nineteen-year-old law student, Robert Lyon, who had fallen in love with a girl named Hughes.

According to a somewhat wistful Justice Riddell, Miss Hughes was "amiable … accomplished … and a young lady of most estimable qualities and high character." She would also show an astonishing capacity to hold a grudge. Her father had died of cholera at Coteau while bringing the family out to the Perth Settlement in 1832, and she and her brother were taken in by a family friend.

While at Perth she received the attentions of young Robert Lyon and became his fiancée. This gossip is something Riddell neglects to mention. What his account does give us is a sketch of a young man eagerly pursuing a law career who, after a few drinks at a dingy Bytown tavern, made a naughty remark about his fiancée to his best friend, John Wilson.

Twenty-one-year-old John Wilson worked out of the same law office as Lyon, and possessed a reputation as someone who abhorred "unchaste conversation." The extent of this abhorrence is suggested in a few lines of Valentine poetry he wrote to the same Miss Hughes:

> Nor words can give me any cause to fear
> Would be offensive to thy modest ear

It seems the modesty of Miss Hughes's ear had assumed almost pathological proportions to Wilson, for he promptly informed her of Robert Lyon's naughty comment. She in turn "disavowed" Robert Lyon, who, in a state of confusion, punched Wilson in the face. Acting on the advice of friends, Wilson challenged Lyons to a duel and the challenge was met.

In a hard rain, on June 13, 1833, the parties assembled in a ploughed field beneath an elm tree. Lyon's initial choice for a second declined and he settled on Henry Le Lievre, a sinister figure who had designs on the young Miss Hughes himself. Since a local census from 1817 shows a population of 709 men to 179 women, it is not inconceivable Le Lievre hoped Wilson and Lyon might conveniently dispatch each other, allowing him to renew his efforts toward the young woman, uncontested.

Both combatants missed on the first fire. Wilson wanted a reconciliation. Le Lievre refused and insisted on another shot. The young man he represented stood in the pouring rain, barely twenty years old, numbed by a broken heart, betrayed by the sanctimonious actions of his best friend, rejected by his fiancée, and seeing the last moments of his life entrusted to an middle-aged rival who possibly wanted him dead.

After the first shots, a surgeon, Dr. Hamilton, attempted to talk Lyon into a reconciliation. Again Le Lievre interfered and insisted the pistols be reloaded. The surgeon then urged the boys to settle. Wilson wanted very much to settle, but Lyon would not. A second round of shots was exchanged and Lyon fell convulsing on the ground, where he died several minutes later.

At the trial, John Wilson and his second were defended by Henry Sherwood, an ambitious speculator who in 1826 had helped Samuel Jarvis heave Mackenzie's typescript in Lake Ontario. In case there might be any doubt about the outcome, the Judge reminded the jury that the practice of private combat had its origin in the high example of kings, and that Wilson had adopted the "only alternative to which men of honour thought open to him ..."

The jury acquitted Wilson, who then married the ex-fiancée of his ex-best friend, moved to St. Thomas, Ontario, and had eight children by her. Affectionately known as "Honest John Wilson," he sentenced seven Fenians to hang in 1867 and occupied a peripheral position on the ruling clique until his death in 1869.

The man who defended him was later accused of being drunk in the street, to which he responded by publishing a pamphlet insisting otherwise. He was defeated as a Toronto alderman in 1851 by John Ridout's brother and died four years later on a Bavarian holiday.

Miss Hughes, not satisfied by the death of her former fiancée, nursed a grudge for the rest of her long life. It is reported that at a very senior age, she spotted a distant relative of the Lyon family on a Toronto streetcar and commenced to violently curse him. Henry Le Lievre skulked into the bush and disappeared from history.

Today, the site of the Perth duel is preserved as a tourist attraction, and has been given the title of "Last Duel Park," which it probably is not. Robert Lyons was, however, the last known

victim of a fatal duel in Ontario. He is buried in an Anglican
cemetery beneath the words:

ROBERT LYON
Student at Law
He fell
in mortal combat
13th of June 1833
in the 20th Year
of his Age
Requiescat in pace

4

Paul Kane:
Disappearing the Red Man

"The Indians are doomed ... having cast aside his useless
snares and shot his last arrow into empty spaces ... he will
lie down upon the snow which will soon cover him as with
a shroud and, with him a whole race will have disappeared
forever from the face of the earth."
— Charles-Hubert Lavollée, Paris, 1859

Paul Kane was born in Mallow, Ireland, in 1810, the early child of a local Irish girl and a British officer stationed there. At the age of nine his family immigrated to the mud village of York, later to be named Toronto. Topped with red hair and distinguished by a pocked face, the young boy spent his childhood spearing jackfish in the reeds of Toronto Island, and running with the young sons of "half breeds," — "bad specimens of the French voyageur," as one writer called them. He played with Indian children among the wigwams at the foot of Yonge Street; a common sight then, and one that vanished entirely during his life.

By his teenage years Paul Kane developed an interest in the local theatrical scene and was in regular attendance at Frank's

Hotel on old King Street. A lone violinist with a patch over one eye provided music to productions of *Lady of the Lake* and *Ali Baba and the Forty Thieves*.

Stepping out of this building on the June 4, 1828, Paul Kane, then eighteen years old, witnessed the drunken street murder of a Quaker. Kane's testimony helped convict the killer, a typesetter employed by William Lyon Mackenzie. On the night of the public hanging, Mackenzie stood next to the young man as the rope was placed around his neck. According to one observer, the revolutionary "wept until his starched white collar was soggy."

Although records prove that Paul Kane was baptized in a parish church at Mallow, County Cork, Ireland, he very early on began to insist that Toronto was his birthplace. As a proud, self-described Canadian he would have felt the tug and the intrigue of the "Nor'West," that storied land beyond Lakes Huron and Superior. It was "a land of perfect freedom," noted Toronto resident Henry Scadding, holding fierce appeal to many young men, even if those same men had no idea "where the Nor'West precisely was" or how to get there.

Whatever influence the northwest exercised over the young Paul Kane, he was, from an early age, an artist. He was soon apprenticing in a furniture factory in Cobourg, Ontario, painting portraits with brushes purchased for him in New York. Later he would go hungry in Naples while studying the classics; Murillo's Madonna in the Corsini Palace was a favourite.

In June 1842, having spent some five years painting portraits in America, he landed in New Orleans, paying his passage down the Mississippi with a sketch of the captain of the riverboat *Norma*, one of the few verifiable Kane productions during this period. September found him in Marseilles. Then Genoa. Then

Rome. Later that same year, he hiked to Naples. Rumours that he sailed from Naples to North Africa are probably unfounded, although one account has him in the company of Syrian explorers on his way to Jerusalem. Late in 1842 he travelled by foot through the Brenner Pass into Switzerland. He later blamed the snow glare from this trip for the onset of his early blindness. From Switzerland he roamed to Paris and then to London, where he encountered the American artist George Caitlin.

Caitlin, a tragic and solitary figure who would soon disappear into the jungles of South America, wrote longingly of the North American Natives: "I love a people ... who are honest without laws. Who have no jails and no poorhouse ... and oh how I love a people who don't live for the love of money." Caitlin painted the Indians of the United States plains and lectured on Indian culture, espousing the popular and widely accepted belief that Indians themselves were facing extinction before the onslaught of European settlers. The role of the artist, insisted Caitlin, was to record this doomed and romantic race before it was wiped out completely.

Paul Kane took Caitlin's message to heart. He would do in the northwest what the American painter had done for the United States. From London he travelled to Toronto (in typical Paul Kane fashion, he arrived via Mobile, Alabama). Then on June 17, 1845, armed with a gun, ammunition, a portfolio, and a box of paints, he started out on what is perhaps the longest and most remarkable journey in the history of painting.

While the Natives of North America have convincingly survived, the environment they lived in, the world Paul Kane travelled through, painted, and wrote about, is substantially changed. No longer are six-hundred-pound sturgeon disgorged on the banks of the Fraser River. Rarely, if ever, does an itinerant painter converse with an Indian who has calmly shot his mother at her own request. "Where precisely did you shoot her" Kane wanted to know. Nor does he eat boiled calf cut from the womb of a buffalo, or dine, as Kane did, on moose lips, moose nose, and buffalo testicles. Kane, it seems, had a preference for buffalo tongue.

He also participated in the last great hunts both as an artist and a hunter, going with two thousand Métis men, women, and children proceeding across the prairie with 1,500 Red River carts in tow. When the hunt was over, each of these carts would be packed with the dried meat of ten buffalo. Through this scene ran the dogs feeding on the offal and remains of the slain animals. Out his window in Fort Edmonton, Kane saw the final herd in all of its enormity. He describes a buffalo shot six times before it "sickened" and then several more times before it finally fell dead. When he put scales to it, he found the head alone weighed 210 pounds. Kane promptly had the head shipped east; one of many trophies he brought back from his life among the North American Indians. Five years later, the last animals of this herd were gone for good. What we have now instead are Kane's paintings, currently hanging in the Art Gallery of Ontario. Given the size of his subject, they are remarkably small canvases, and strangely static; the technical demands of motion and speed eluded him to the end. Yet visually, in its bare-bones depiction, this is what it must have looked like: countless tiny buffalo, pursued by the even tinier figures on horseback.

On his mythic journey from east to west, Paul Kane saw things that few people would ever see again. He encountered white men who had opened the flap of a medicine tent and been blinded by what they saw there. He travelled with carriers of sacred pipe stems. He suffered the agonies of frostbite and *mal de racquet* (snowshoe sickness), cured by slicing open the calf muscles with a knife, or scorching them with a burned stick. On a desperate trail in the Rockies, Kane witnessed a horse sidle up to another horse and help support its pack across *its own back*. He endured eighty-seven consecutive days in a canoe, and traded away a rain coat made from the intestines of seals. In an often-reproduced picture he sketched a Flathead woman restructuring the skull of her infant. He befriended an Esquimaux who was 110 years old and had suckled his son with his own breast milk after his wife died in childbirth. He watched people urinate on walnuts to flavour them, and in the pre-photographic world of 1845, he watched the course of history change, sometimes for the price of a plug of tobacco. At one point in his journey, in need of favourable wind, he was approached by an Ojibway medicine man who offered to provide it. The bargain was simple: six days of favourable wind in exchange for one plug of tobacco. Kane made the deal and was amused when he got his favourable wind.

At one point, in a remarkable display of generosity, he was allowed to wander freely among the tribal burial grounds of the Indian dead. He was warned beforehand that to steal one bone would mean his immediate death. Despite these warnings, he stole a skull and kept it hidden beneath the dog-hair blankets and his buffalo robe. According to Paul Kane's wife, her husband was "risking his life" for science. Today, of course, this is called something very different.

Paul Kane returned to Toronto in October 1848, after nearly four years of wandering North America. He soon mounted an exhibition that was enthusiastically received and provided Canadians with their first panoramic glance at the western terrain and the Native peoples who inhabited it. He single-mindedly devoted the next twenty years to the rendering of his sketches and the promotion of himself and his work. He became the first Canadian artist to get a grant from the government. He was eulogized for two hours in the Canadian Parliament. That same government threatened him with a lawsuit in order to receive their paintings. He produced the first large, coloured lithograph in Canada, but was unable to sell it. He was the first of many to say, "Canada is no place for an artist." His contemporary, Cornelius Krieghoff, was so appalled with the state of Canadian art that he considered it "no wonder our men should be drunkards and our girls flirts."

Paul Kane married, had four children, and, in an effort to support himself, wrote or had ghost-written his *Wanderings of an Artist Among the Indians of North America*. Since he was almost incapable of spelling, the text was transcribed by his wife, Harriet Clench, the daughter of a Cobourg furniture maker, an accomplished painter herself. In 1858, he sailed to England and placed his manuscript with Longmans of London. Annoyed by the delays, Kane marched into the prestigious office, confronted Longman, and uttered the speech that every author yearns to make: "I am independent of the world. Give me my manuscript. I am returning to Canada." Longman refused, the book was published, and the English edition sold out immediately.

Eventually, after twenty years of hard work, Paul Kane left behind him a visual record of almost unbelievable proportions. In the sweep of this achievement, he rendered North America from a Toronto brewery to the eruption of Mount St. Helen's, from wampum belts at Mackinac to Chinook canoe burials at the Cowlitz River and Ojibway grave houses on Georgian Bay. He sketched the medicine pipe stem dance of the Blackfoot, rendered hurried portraits at Michipicoten, Manitowaning, at Spokane, on the Saugeen River, at Puget Sound. He drew Chinook lodges, Klickitat lodges, Clallam travelling lodges, medicine masks of the northwest coast tribes, and salmon fishing on the Columbia River. He sketched the last massive buffalo hunts and he painted portraits of Nez Perce Indians, the Walla Walla, the Assininboin, the Cree, and others of the more than eighty tribes that he encountered.

Despite these achievements, the land that he so extensively wandered through proved elusive to him. His finished paintings show the familiar hues of a European apprenticeship. A palate of greens and browns clouds his canvases. He knew what he called "the brilliant sky so peculiar to North America," and yet he painted European skies in their stead, grand, dark, and romantic. In his portrait of *Cunnawa-bum*, a Cree half-breed woman at Fort Edmonton, his subject peers out with too much coyness and coquetry from behind a fan made of a swan's wing. Exotic, with exquisite fingernails, she is a pampered European debutante rendered with a touch of Indian eroticism. Her face was chosen for the cover of Kane's book.

By the 1930s, it was reluctantly conceded that Native populations in Canada were increasing rapidly both on and off the reserve and had been for some time. With this finding, "the vanishing race" assumption of the previous century was laid to rest. With it was also exposed the perplexing difficulty posed by the legacy of Paul Kane. As late as the 1970s, commentators still praised his work as "an ethnologically rich series of paintings of Indians from a day when their culture was still *comparatively pure.*" Kane sometimes requested his subjects dress in more "authentic" garments. In this demand for purity, white observers denied what is perhaps the greatest achievement of First Nations' culture: the ability to change and negotiate, to choose and adapt, to transform, incorporate, improvise, to withstand famine, ice, smallpox, tuberculosis, residential schools, even Hollywood. It denies their right to move to the next stage of history.

Today, at the Art Gallery of Ontario, several small Kane paintings hang on the wall. In one, *Indian Encampment at Georgian Bay,* an Indian man reclines on the ground. He seems only moments away from extinction. His face is painted red. How could Paul Kane know the concept of the "red man" was born after European fishermen encountered east coast Natives who had daubed their faces with red dye? His audience expected red men, so Kane gave them red men. Next to him is a woman pounding at a churn, an activity destined for oblivion. Scattered everywhere are the celebrated birch-bark canoes, displayed as if for the last time. Everything in this painting feels forced to the brink of oblivion. The carefully rendered canoes already belong in a museum, yet even as Kane painted them they were fast becoming the most common vessel on the waters of North America. Today, if a technology threatens the supremacy of the canoe, it's another Native invention, the kayak.

Above this painting hangs a second small canvas depicting buffalo. Their dark forms sprawl on the prairies, for the last time. The Indians, the buffalo, there is hardly a difference between the two. The palate of this canvas is so dark, so brooding, it is barely possible to see what the painting is *of.*

Today, Paul Kane is regarded as one if not *the* father of Canadian painting, and the first tourist to make it as far as the Rocky Mountains. Yet as a person he remains almost invisible. He was a hard-working, brusque individual. His paintings when measured against his great contemporary, Cornelius Krieghoff, appear humourless, his palette is grim in comparison to Krieghoff's, and lacks most noticeably his stunning reds. Like many, he shared a common fascination with the North American Native. Beyond this, it is difficult to get a sense of the man. Only several photographs exist; one shows Paul Kane returned from the west dressed in full Native regalia, his right hand splayed assertively on his hip. It is an uncomfortable photograph. Kane himself looks uncomfortable. It is also difficult not to sense the confusion in the man's face, a weariness, and sadness, his eyes narrow and sideways as if attempting to see something that has passed him by.

A few hints of the man are to be found in his personal library, known to contain, among others, six volumes of Shakespeare, eleven volumes of Bell's British Theatre, *Remarks On Italy*, Henry Schoolcraft's *The Indian In His Wigwam*, and perhaps most significantly, Mrs. Dall's *A Woman's Right to Labour*. Retiring and irascible, he had, in the words of a friend, "turned into a bear with a sore head." When conversations stopped being of interest to him, he lapsed into silence and refused to utter a word. "An ungodly man of not much learning," is how one female observer described him (although she did admit he was very knowledgeable about birds). The painter Frederick Verner, who years later followed in Kane's western footsteps, tells how, as a boy, he summoned up his courage, knocked on Paul Kane's studio door, and bravely requested drawing lessons. According to Verner, the great master, without speaking a word, shut the door in his face.

In this gesture we get another brief glimpse of Paul Kane. He is an artist behind a shut door, engaged in a single-minded quest to render half the continent of North America, racing against time and his own failing eyesight. By 1860, barely fifty years old, his vision seriously debilitated, he gave up his studio and stopped painting. Toward the end of his life, he took long daily rambles across the Toronto Islands, returning at night on the last ferry. Already forgotten in the bustle of expanding Canada, Paul Kane was now just an aging man who moved too slowly for the next generation as they charged eagerly over the gangplanks. They had no way of knowing that this bearded and apparently inconsequential figure had taken a legendary journey west and heard the first languages spoken from the mouths of the first peoples. He had seen things no one would ever see again, watched herds of buffalo stomp in terror across the plains. All the while, with sketchbook in hand, he tried to render the face of a continent as it uttered what he could only presume was its last unique and full-blooded cry. He was there in the last extraordinary days of "contact" when one civilization had stumbled roughshod into another. He sketched it, painted it, collected it, and later wrote about it. For better or worse, Canadian art just about begins with these sketches and paintings.

In the winter of 1871, following a lengthy walk, Paul Kane died at home in Toronto. He was sixty-one years old.

II

On Febuary 6, 2002, a small Paul Kane painting, *Scene in the Northwest,* sold at auction in Toronto for more than five million dollars. This was, by far, the largest sum of money ever paid for a painting by a Canadian artist, or for any work of art executed on Canadian soil.

Today the painting hangs on the second floor of the Art Gallery of Ontario. It is a small work and portrays Captain John Henry Lefroy, a career soldier and a scientist who had come to Canada to study terrestrial magnetism, and whose calculations would eventually ascertain the site of the magnetic north pole. While in Canada, Captain Lefroy also founded Toronto's first book club.

This man dominates the painting. Almost equally dominant is the toboggan on which his mighty instruments of science have been carefully wrapped and secured. A brooding and somewhat foreign sky fills the top of the canvas and Leroy's assistant stands stiffly in the very centre of the painting. His back is turned to the viewer; this posture is explained by the fact that this man was not in Toronto at the time Kane worked on the painting, and unable to pose for the painter. Far to the left, beneath two stunted and disfigured pine tree are the subjects of his artistic enterprise, "the North American Indians." Painted in advance of Kane's great western journey, the canvas suggests that the matter of priorities has already been decided. Yes, there are North American Indians in this work. If the viewer looks carefully two can be seen, lolling in apparent sloth, the man, if that is what he is, lying on his belly in the open flap of a sagging wigwam; the woman is dressed in a colourless robe. They are faceless, pushed too far into the background to warrant a face. They seem almost physically banished, confined to the very fringes of the painting. They are substantially smaller and less significant than the two eager dogs who wait to pull the Captain's toboggan and his implements of science. As to those two barely rendered Native viewers, they watch in awe as the great enterprise of science and discovery unfolds around them. They have been all but disappeared, literally and physcially marginalized.

When the auction house, Sotheby's, published the 2002 Canadian catalogue with this painting on the cover, the faceless North American Indians were cropped from the picture.

5

A Brief History of Trees

In 1836, an unhappily married woman named Anna Jameson took a ramble through the New World. When it was over, she did what most travellers to Canada did: she wrote a book about it. This work, which has entered the Canadian canon and become a classic, contains a frequently quoted sentence: "A Canadian Settler hates a tree, regards it as his natural enemy, as something to be destroyed, eradicated, annihilated by all and any means."

In fairness to Mrs. Jameson, Canadian settlers were definitely *not* tree huggers. They had their own attitudes toward trees and they had their reasons for having them. By 1822, the Military Settling Department had determined the tree to be a leading cause of death in the new world. "Drowned, deceased," and "killed by a tree," were fingered as the great culprits of Canadian depopulation. The first, of course, was "Gone to the States."

To be killed by a tree was not unusual. Often, as happened to the Reverend John Scadding, the tree fell on you. More typically the axe-head bounced and cleaved a foot or leg, leading to the most frequent injury in Canadian medical history: the hatchet wound. The Jesuit Menard, one of the first white men to reach

Lake Superior, had a tree fall on him while paddling a canoe. In the timber camps of eastern Ontario, lumbermen stricken by typhoid and diphtheria were typically carried out in the blankets they died in and buried in a ditch. Sometimes they had a tooth pulled by a camp dentist and died of infection. There were countless ways to be killed by a tree. Even the Iroquois Book of Rites, which predates Columbus by half a century, congratulates all who have survived wild beasts … thorny ways and falling trees.

Most famously, death by trees comes in the form of fire. There is barely a town, settlement, ship, or even a lighthouse in the Dominion that did not burn to the ground or waterline at least once (and often twice). One of the first ordinances passed in English Canada was a law requiring homeowners to keep a pail of water on the porch at all times. When Toronto burned to the ground for the second time, wood, as a building material, was outlawed in favour of brick. Vancouver was destroyed by an 1886 fire that reduced the entire city to ashes in less than forty-five minutes; one witness stated the city did not so much burn as "explode." Ottawa burned twice and the mill that sawed the boards that built Ottawa burned four times. The mining town of Cochrane burned three times. More than two hundred people lost their lives in the 1916 fire. An equal number, caught out in the backwoods, are also believed to have died. Ships on the Great Lakes, blinded by smoke from forest fires, have plunged against rock shores and been wrecked.

Some of the fires that ravaged the Ottawa valley blotted out the sun for days. These were the "crown fires" that exploded the crown of the trees, raced down the trunk to the bush floor, and went after the next one. Logging practices of the day left one third of every tree behind, making the forest floor a tinderbox. The great fires moved over it at eight miles an hour, hopping over bodies of water as wide as the Ottawa River. Some fires stretched seventy miles across, with flames, fuelled by the rich flammable resins of the pine, shooting up a 150 feet into the air. Dirt itself was known to ignite.

A 1948 forest fire that swept Superior's north shore generated so much smoke that streetlights had to be turned on at noon — *in Texas*. It is not unknown for smoke from Canadian forest fires to reach England. The Great Miramichi Fire of 1825 has been called "the most dreadful conflagration ... in the history of the world!" Five hundred people died. It stretched seventy miles on either side of the Miramichi River and caused winds of such velocity that salmon were sucked out of the river and scattered in the trees.

Given this grim history, it is perhaps not surprising that Canadians were ambivalent toward trees. For Christian settlers, there was a much deeper reason to distrust trees; Christ was crucified on a tree: a trembling aspen. The very reason the aspen trembles, says Thomas De Quincey, is because *it knows* Christ was murdered on its back.

Mixing trees with religion is a long and honoured tradition. Native Gods blow on trees to make them grow. In the past, skilled Natives could routinely make a rope of willow branches and lasso the moon. To Pope Paul VI, the Christian church is a tree, "a great tree ... she puts down her roots in a variety of social and human terrains." To the poet, the breath of God does not just sigh in the trees, it *soughs*. This delightful Anglo-Saxon word pronounced either "sows" or "suffs" originates from the lost verb *swogan*, "to sound." Grey Owl, the world's most famous fake Indian, and Canada's original conservationist, called this the sound of trees "praying to be saved" from the timberman. In what is perhaps the first ecological manifesto written in Canada,

Grey Owl pinned a note to a tree that said, "God made the forest for the animals. Don't burn it up and make it look like hell."

Felling large trees was not easy in pioneer times. John Galt once discovered an oak tree in southern Ontario that was thirty-six feet in diameter, with branches that started eighty feet above the ground. He speculated the only reason it remained alive was because "there was not yet a saw in Canada long enough to cut through it." The beech trees of Christian Island were once so large they had to be drilled and brought down with dynamite before being fitted into a sawmill. Today the Sitkas of British Columbia are sometimes flown out, individually, by helicopter.

For many years it was said and believed that the Canadian forest stretched to infinity. Even those who should have known better, such as Stephen Leacock, an economist, described with confidence the "trees flowing in from the inexhaustible northern backwoods." In private, the timber barons predicted two hundred years of full cutting. Arguably, they got forty. In those forty years the largest pinery on the planet was cut down and shipped east on a hundred different rivers. It was an act that staggers the imagination, cost the lives of an untold number of men, and was perhaps as grandiose and labour-intensive as the building of the great pyramids of Egypt or putting a spaceship on the moon.

In those brief years, there appeared on the earth an apotheosis of wood, a technology based on trees which today is almost impossible to imagine. When rivers proved insufficient for transporting cut logs, artificial rivers — timber slides — were built above ground. These structures sometimes ran forty miles in length. The men who built them lived in shanties constructed of the trees around them. Watertight scoop roofs were made from halved logs. Door hinges were carved from pine. Nails to hold wood together were made from wood. Timber trains ran on rails made of — timber. Fully half the men in Canada were employed cutting down trees.

An entire country had sprung up based on the removal of trees; the pine tree in particular. This country within a country soon developed its own history, its code of ethics, a repertoire of song, of poetry, even its own language. Some of the more renowned examples of timber jargon surviving today are "jackpot," the heap of filthy clothing the timbermen left behind them at the end of the season, and "bushwacker": an itinerant timberman who roved from camp to camp, in the sense of spreading lice. To "fly off the handle" had much more serious consequences in the timberfields than it does around the dinner table. The term "widow maker" has its origins in the Canadian bush where it describes a dead but standing tree; also known by the French-Canadian word *chicot*, which corrupted into *cheeko*, a term still heard to describe a large stump.

The insularity of this language is sounded in the following exchange between an injured timberman and a nurse. The timberman, a man named Happy Murphy (apparently it was *de rigeur* for all timbermen to have nicknames) is asked by the nurse how the accident happened. He replies,

> "Well you see, I was the skyman, and we were shy a grounder, and there was a gazaboo come down the pike and the push took him on. The first thing he sent up was a big blue butt, and I yelled out to him to throw a Saginaw into her, but he St. Croixed her, and then he gunned her, and she came up and cracked my stern."
>
> "I don't understand," said the nurse.
>
> "I don't either," interrupted the top loader. "I think he must have been bughouse or jigerood."

Behind such displays of rhetoric lay the elimination of the North American forest. By 1890, Wisconsin was practically denuded of trees and American timber barons were buying up timber rights in Canada where the policy of "cut out and get out" was in full swing. By 1920, the spoliation of the Lake Superior forests was complete. Stumpage fees were neither collected nor assessed, and the trees often went straight into American mills.

Apparently one of the first efforts at timber management undertaken by the Canadian forest industry occurred in 1865 when assassins were hired to murder E. Pauline Johnson's father, the forest warden who resolutely guarded the trees of the Six Nations reserve. By the early twentieth century, the industry was so corrupt that Port Arthur became known as "the place where they manufacture affidavits." When the Ontario Temperance Act came into effect and it was no longer possible for hotel owners to make a killing in liquor, they found it an easy move into timbering.

By 1919, the "timber thieves" had created such havoc that the Riddell-Latchford Timber Commission was appointed to investigate. A timberman accused of cutting trees on private property offered the intriguing defence that trees belonged to God, therefore he could do what he wanted with them. When a piling and pulpwood operator was asked by the commission what he would do if he saw good timber on private land, he answered at once, "I'd wheel right into her."

Wheel right in, they did. J.R. Booth took a million trees out of the Algonquin area a year, and did not plant a single one in return. His mill at Ottawa, the largest in the world, churned out a million board feet a shift. The largest sawmill in the United States at Duluth did not produce that much lumber in a year. A century after Philemon Wright had guided the first crib of pine trees down the Ottawa River in 1807, the cry was already ringing through the great eastern pinery: "Crooked trees make straight dollars, boys. Cut them down!"

By 1922, the Riddell-Latchford Timber Commission wrapped up its investigations with a series of recommendations that were ignored. In 1925, J.R. Booth transported the last squared timber out of eastern Ontario and then died at the age of ninety-nine. The great pineries of eastern Canada were gone.

It was a different story in western Canada. Here, the compulsion to rid the land of trees was replaced by the equally potent urge to plant them. To the European, arriving in a land without trees was a second form of exile — from the biblical garden that trees symbolize. What followed in the west was an effort to re-establish Eden on a treeless plain. The apple tree was preferred; the first tree in the first garden, a potent Christian symbol, a good food source, and an act of faith and permanence, as an apple tree can take years to yield. The first apple trees to reach the Okanagan Valley were planted by a Catholic priest, Father Charles Pandosy, in 1862. Pandosy, a devout, wise-cracking Oblate who enjoyed nothing better than rolling up the sleeves of his robes and getting in a good fist fight, is sometimes called the Canadian Johnny Appleseed.

Generally, apple trees were planted without success by the hundreds of thousands until the Saunder's Hybrid proved capable of surviving a prairie winter. The planting of trees became a moral passion. In the nineteenth century, in the United States and Canada, a special "Arbor Day" was "set apart and consecrated" for the planting of trees.

Whether we know it or not, trees are a standard for judging distances. We form our sense of space in relation to a tree. In southern

Ontario, a mature hardwood is the size of a three-storey house. Its mantle fans over the roof in summer and provides a windbreak in winter. Many of the neighbourhoods of North America are arranged on this principle.

The visual standard set by trees accounts for the disorientation experienced on the prairies: the sense that things look closer than they are. In the Arctic, where the tree is replaced by the rock, the feeling can be reversed: points that seem far away are closer. Near the Arctic Circle, I heard an Inuk woman boast of being "down South." Curious as to how far she'd managed to get, I asked her. "Whitehorse," she said. When I suggested Whitehorse might not qualify as "down south," she laughed at me. "Of course it does. They have trees there and *everything*!"

Trees define this continent just as the removal of trees defines its deterioration. Thoreau, in a passage almost too cruel to read, once described an axe head cleaving into a tree trunk as though it were an assault on the human body. When John Galt cut down the first tree at what is now Guelph, Ontario, he observed, tellingly, "the genius of the Woods departing this place forever." Author Malcolm Lowry's favourite tree outside Vancouver was cut down in order that a small part could be used to build a violin. Incensed, Lowry pinned a note to the stump, reading, "Would you like this to happen to you, you pig dog? When you hear your lousy fiddle it will make a noise like slaughtered birds." According to Oliver Wendell Holmes, the best poems he ever wrote were the trees he planted on the banks of the Housatonic River. The painter John Constable embraced trees the way he embraced children. In his memoirs, Emerson hoped that all the pages of his books would bear the smell of pine. Author W.G. Sebald describes a village priest, who, on a certain day each year, gave a speech to the village trees.

It would seem that in our deepest imagination, the tree constitutes a human being. When John Galt and his party felled that maple at Guelph, "there was a funereal pause as when a coffin is lowered into the grave." The killing of trees creates outrage and the planting of seedlings is hailed as virtuous. The conflict resonates throughout the language of timbering. According to the industry, trees are "harvested." But the term has not stuck. Trees are "cut down," "felled," "chopped down." It is the language of warfare: the warrior who falls in battle, men who are "cut down" by machine-gun fire.

Whether it be the Tree of Life, painted fifteen thousand years ago on a Canaanite Megiddo vase, the tree of knowledge, the inverted tree of the Cabala, the Iroquois Tree of Peace, or the Green Man mythologies that reach back to the last ice age, trees are "rooted" so deeply in us that it is difficult to know where the tree ends and where the human begins. According to Pauline Johnson, her parents resolved their squabbles by walking among the hardwoods of the Grand River — the first known example of a successful couples' therapy performed by trees. These massive maples, elms, walnuts and oaks were in her words, "the imperial trees ... voiceful and kingly." Here is sounded the familiar notion of the tree as natural king. The white pine has long been called "the Monarch of the Forest." Trees have "crowns." For centuries we have attributed wisdom to them. Christ may have been crucified on a tree, but the Buddha became enlightened while sitting beneath one.

The study of trees is known as dendrology. The tree, according to Messrs. Morton and Lewis, is defined rather unsatisfactorily as "a single stemmed perennial woody plant growing to a height of more than 10 feet." Trees, like people and animals, migrate. Spruces, larches, birches, poplars, and willows sweep quickly across a continent. Oaks, walnuts, and butternuts possess heavy seeds and require animals to move them, hence they travel slower. Regardless of their speed, all trees, according to Vladimir Nabokov, "are pilgrims, all trees in the world are journeying somewhere. They have their Messiah whom they seek." Perhaps that messiah lives in Toronto, which occasionally subtitles itself the City of Trees.

There are approximately 130 native species of trees in North America. Each of them possesses its own Book of Wisdom. This wisdom was accumulated over many centuries by the First People, who, fortunately, were willing to pass it on.

When Cartier arrived on the shores of North America in the 1530s with half his crew dying of scurvy, the Stadaconans supplied them with the boiled young twigs of the red spruce that were mixed with maple sugar and fermented. The knowledge that this concoction cured scurvy could not have come easily, or overnight. Untold years of trial and error were needed to discover whether the *young* twigs, not the mature ones, did the job, or that maple sugar and not sturgeon eggs was required for the concoction to work.

That the Natives possessed such knowledge was recognized early on by the Europeans who witnessed "Indians" extracting syrup from the maple tree as early as the 1600s. In 1824, the Reverend William Bell, in his book *Hints to Immigrants*, advised using trees as a cure for being lost: "large trees have always moss on the north side and the largest limbs generally on the south." According to Bell, Indians steered their way through the woods by following the longest branches of the birch tree, "which are said to point eastward."

It would not take long to observe Natives using the white ash to relieve the itching of mosquito bites. Or to learn that the roots of the eastern cottonwood were excellent for creating friction fires. South Ontario settlers were soon using dried beech leaves to stuff mattresses because it was springier than straw. Canadian pine, it was discovered, does not warp and gutter in the rain, which made it perfect for the masts of sailing ships and the windowsills of houses. In the absence of writing paper, the French explorer La Hontain took to inscribing his notes on birchbark. For the constipated, the white walnut tree provides a soothing laxative. The inner root of the tulip tree makes an excellent heart stimulant, although it not clear how this connection was made, or by whom. The same can be said of the witch hazel, which is used to divine water. Rope was made from the hackberry tree and ink from the pin oak. Arrow shafts from the western snowberry, bows from the yew and ash. The acorns of the white oak can be eaten — the oil extracted from it soothes painful joints. Rocky Mountain juniper was found to be excellent for the manufacture of pencils and the black willow for polo balls. The letters in Gutenberg's printing press were carved from beech. And on it goes.

Perhaps the Vikings had the final word when they insisted the world was held the world together by a tree: the ash tree.

By 1860, southern Ontario was almost denuded of trees. Anna Jameson's tree-hating (and penniless) Canadians had chopped down everything in sight and burned it. A contemporary, Samuel Strickland, once described the countryside of southwestern Ontario lit up night after night by as many as two hundred brush fires. The ash from these burnings would be rendered into potash, a cash crop, and sold to England to make soap. Perhaps in uttering her famous comment, Jameson was unaware that the government of Upper Canada demanded that settlers clear a certain acreage of trees each year or face having their land repossessed.

After spending barely a year in the New World, during which time she made hateful comments about the Irish, inaccurate and problematic observations on the "Indians," and condescending remarks about Canadian settlers, Anna Jameson concluded that "the people here are in great enthusiasm about me," then returned to England where she wrote books about art and died in 1860.

Five years later, paid assassins attacked Pauline Johnson's father, the officially appointed protector of the "imperial" hardwoods of the Grand River. Attacked again a decade later, he finally died in his own bed beneath the oaks and the walnuts that suffed and soughed outside his window. He was just one of many who were killed by trees. He died not for his hatred of them, but for his love and his devotion; one of many martyrs who have given their life to this complex and barely understood religion.

6

Pauline Johnson:
A Thousand Measures of Mother Love

Nine miles southeast of Brantford, Ontario, on the east bank of the Grand River, stands a somewhat neglected colonial mansion covered in cracked stucco. The house is built among the walnut trees and hardwoods on land belonging to the Iroquois Confederacy and is peculiar in that it possesses two front doors; one faces east, the other west. These doors are identical and represent an example of Iroquois diplomacy at its finest.

Through these doors two societies entered and dealt with each other. To the eastern door facing the road came the emissaries of England, artists, administrators and royalty, from Sir Garnet Wolseley to the Marquis of Lorne. They climbed from carriages, curious and carrying gifts. Through the other door, facing the river, came the Iroquois; their canoes hauled safely up the bank, also bearing gifts, also filled with curiosity.

The house, which no European or Native ever entered or left by the back door, belonged to Mohawk Chieftain George Henry Martin Johnson. A Christianized Indian, he spoke fluent English, German, French, Mohawk, Oneida, Seneca, Onondaga, Tuscarora, and Cayuga, and for his entire life refused to wear

gloves, believing he breathed through his hands. A blood relative
of Hiawatha, his own father, Chief "Smoke" Johnson had fought
with distinction in the major campaigns of the 1812 war, and was
the only man left on the Brantford reserve capable of deciphering
the wampum belts. He was also said to be the last man alive who
could translate each word of the Iroquois Book of Rites.

In the mid 1850s, Chief George Johnson fell in love with a
young Scottish woman named Emily Susanna Howells, and, in
the face of tribal and parental opposition, married her. In doing
so, he forfeited the right to pass on his title to a future son, a right
his family had possessed for six hundred years. The Howell family was also unimpressed and the young lovers found it necessary
to travel east to Kingston to marry. According to an account the
priest "cantered through the service in Latin, pronounced the
benediction in English, and congratulated the couple in Indian."

The unusual pair returned to the reserve near Brantford and settled in the white colonial house with two front doors. George
Johnson resumed his duties as chief and government translator
for the Six Nations confederacy and spent his spare time walking the exquisite walnut groves with his wife. It was said no two
people "in the history of the world" had been so perfectly mated.
Whatever rare spats flared between them were resolved by one
of them making flattering comments about the trees. It was
those same trees that would eventually cause the death of Chief
George Johnson.

By the 1860s, the timber trade combined with pioneer
burnings for settlement and potash had left southern Canada
almost treeless. The finest remaining stands of hardwoods were
located on Iroquois lands fringing the Grand River, and it was
here the timber merchants descended. With judicious trading,

a quart of bad whiskey could be exchanged for six dollars worth of rare hardwood.

To combat these encroachments, the government armed George Johnson with the title of Forest Warden and gave him a pistol. He so effectively patrolled his land that liquor traders and timber merchants attempted to assassinate him. Johnson's fearlessness caused even his father, the decorated warrior, to urge him to change tactics. One night he was attacked by nine men who crushed his skull with a lead plumb, kicked him repeatedly in the face, head and back, and left him for dead in a swamp. Somehow he gained consciousness and staggered a mile before meeting a friend who tried to assist him. It is said Chief Johnson rejected this help, worried his wife would be upset if she saw him being aided to the door. For several months he lay in bed. His upper and lower jaws were splintered, his arms and legs broken. A silver dollar could be fitted into a hole in his back.

In 1873, he was again attacked, this time by six men armed with hand spikes. They knocked out his teeth, shattered his hands, broke three ribs, shot him with his own pistol, and dragged him into the middle of the road to die. He did not die. His assailants were captured and spent five years in the Kingston Gaol. Public sympathy swung toward the chief, whose health was entirely broken. He died in his wife's arms in 1884. According to one of his daughters "Cold had settled in all the broken places of his poor body and he slipped away from her ..."

That daughter was Emily Pauline Johnson. She was one of four children born in that house with two front doors. Growing up, her food was served to her on silver trays by servants. In 1871, asked by a friend of her parents what she wanted from the city, the nine-year-old girl answered immediately, "Verses." By the age of twelve she had read heavily in Shakespeare, Emerson, Byron, Scott, and Longfellow.

Her first poem was published in 1884 in a New York magazine. The first public reading of her work took place the next year in Brantford at the unveiling of the Brant Memorial. Said to be too shy to read it herself, it was recited by a local businessman who pronounced the poem "creditable alike to the young Indian poetess and the race for whom she speaks." A Toronto reporter was less impressed, but conceded that Miss Pauline Johnson was "a pleasant-looking Indian maiden," to which she responded with a piece of private doggerel:

No compliment on her I'll laden
She's but a pleasant-looking maiden.

Encouraged by Toronto reporter Frank Yeigh (Johnson, with a love for nicknames, labelled him Yeigh-man), she gave her first public recital at the Young Men's Liberal Club of Ontario in Toronto in 1892. Desperately stage-frightened, she recited her Riel Rebellion poem, "A Cry from an Indian Wife," and stole the show. A veteran soldier of that campaign later approached her and said her poem had left him "ashamed" of the part he'd played in the conflict. She was rebooked a week later as "the Indian Poetess," a title later changed to "the Mohawk Princess."

In 1892, Pauline Johnson was thirty-one years old. She had been writing poetry for seven years and had earned herself three dollars. Her father was dead, her mother, unable to afford the upkeep of the family home, now lived in a small house in Brantford.

Without an income, Pauline Johnson did something that was very unlikely for a woman of her class in the nineties: she earned a living. By early 1892, vaudeville was going strong in both the United States and Canada, and she found a touring partner in Owen Smiley, who was barely in his twenties. For Johnson, this was a new experience. Chaste and naive, she had reportedly never seen a man even partially undressed and had once bragged of having never allowed a man to touch "her hand." She now shared a dressing room with a twenty-two-year-old British homosexual, professional elocutionist, comic, musician, and music-hall entertainer, known for his ability to imitate Scottish bagpipes, and whose most beloved stage piece was titled "Major McStrynger's Mechanical Arm." The two of them began to tour together and in 1893 gave over 125 recitals in fifty different towns. Within two years, Johnson was described by the *New York Sun* as "perhaps the most unique figure in the literary world on this continent."

In the same year a friend insisted she was debasing herself and her poetry with her onstage recitals. Johnson agreed that she was engaging in "brain debasement" … "I sneer at my own littleness in doing so," she wrote. All of it, she insisted, was necessary to finance a book of poems. In April 1894, having earned enough money, she boarded a steamer for London.

Armed with a half-dozen letters of recommendation, and aided by the Canadian High Commissioner, she somehow found her way into the salons and social evenings of London, England. Soon this bold and strikingly beautiful woman from a reserve in southern Ontario was putting on her Indian dress (complete with the scalps of several Hurons) and reciting her poems to ladies, lords and marquises. "I was at a large dinner party," she wrote home, "and wore a very fine gown and was taken to dinner by Mr. Somebody. I forget his name. I talked politics and told them there was no government existing save the confederated government of the Iroquois."

II

Having placed her manuscript *The White Wampum* with The Bodley Head publishing house, she returned to Brantford in July. She and her partner immediately resumed their recital tours, and Pauline Johnson crossed the Rockies for the first time in her life. Somewhere en route she described herself morosely as "the doll of the people and a slave to money." In 1895, in what was to become a familiar theme, a critic for the *St. Thomas Evening Journal* suggested she stop "masquerading as a poetess." *The White Wampum* appeared in July, and was warmly met by Canadian reviewers. British critics found nothing in it worth quoting. Typically, Johnson became upset only when a newspaperman wrongly referred to her as a Bostonian. "God forgive the slanderers," she wrote.

In 1896, for reasons unknown, her partnership with Owen Smiley broke up. A year later she teamed up with Walter McRaye, whom she nicknamed "Dink." Again she began stumping Canada, this time with a second-rate song-and-dance man about whom a critic would say "the only stage he was fit for travelled at about five miles an hour." According to a contemporary entertainer Peggy Webly, she was once introduced to a Manitoba audience with the words: "Now friends, before Miss Johnson's exercises begin, I want you all to remember that Injuns, like us, is folks."

In Winnipeg in 1897, she received a proposal of marriage from a local businessman, accepted it, and was later publicly jilted. Johnson's only surviving comment on this episode is condensed quietly into a line and a half;

My heart forgot its love of God for you,
And you forget me …

In the course of her hectic recital schedule she contracted erysipelas in Orillia and nearly died. It was erysipelas (brain fever), brought on by the severe beatings, that had killed her father. Johnson lost her hair, lamented briefly "my scarred face and cropped hair," and began to perform in wigs that severely irritated her scalp. Eventually she changed the wigs for a hat. "No one suspects the tragedy underneath," she wrote. By 1901 the *Ottawa Citizen* found her performances "mechanical." The *Slocan Drill* had had enough of these "tiresome and monotonous … two horse shows."

Her second book of poems, *Canadian Born*, appeared in 1903. Its dedication read: "White race and Red are one if they are but Canadian Born." Typically, the book contains a portrait of Johnson in Indian dress (just as typically she posed in profile to emphasize her Indian-ness). The book was given, in her words, a most scathing roast, to which she replied gamely, "Well, I must try a novel now, and get criticized."

In 1904, she undertook an extraordinary nine-hundred-mile buggy trip up and back down the Cariboo Trail. With the exception of several miners' wives and prostitutes, she was perhaps the only woman of her generation to do this. There, she witnessed the astonishing flashpoint in history called "the frontier," and the remaining few years of her life would be profoundly affected by it.

In 1906, she returned again to London, England, where she dazzled a doting Swinburne and thrilled a packed audience at Steinway Hall. She was invited by a British newspaper magnate to contribute articles to the *Daily Express*. The most intriguing of these pieces, "A Pagan in St. Paul's Cathedral," shows Johnson, full of her Canadian-born pride, comparing the great cathedral music to "the far-off cadences of the Sault Sainte Marie rapids." The piece has a strangely modern feel to it. London is shown to be a pale substitute for the North, for the Indian Nation, and for Canada. For Johnson, even the great stone structures of London appear trite compared to the craftwork performed on an Indian reserve near Brantford, Ontario, where the stones "take the polish by fingers dipped in sturgeon oil, and long days of friction with fine sand and deer hide."

She returned to Ontario in the winter of 1907. She was now writing almost exclusively short stories and articles about idealized mothers — Indian mothers in particular. A month later she inexplicably crossed the Atlantic and returned to London, England. She did not attempt to place her manuscripts and did not perform. It has been suggested that an unknown love interest accounted for this curious jaunt, although it is equally possible that Pauline Johnson, now forty-six and sensing her impending illness, was looking for a place to die. She did not find it in England. Returning to New York in June 1907, she and McRaye embarked on another breathless circuit tour, this time of the United States. Typically she found herself stomping the boards with such celebrities as Miss Elma B. Smith, the "delightful child impersonator and bird warbler." By October she was back in Winnipeg, preparing for a western tour. She and McRaye performed throughout 1908 on the western prairies. By April she was touring the Maritimes. In Saint John, a local church ladies group presented her with ten dollars as appreciation from "all women who strive for a name and place in this Canada of ours." By the end of June she was in Vancouver, resting, and writing commercial work for family magazines. During this period she also started work on the forgotten but remarkable essay, "My Mother."

She and McRaye toured the Maritimes before Pauline Johnson headed west alone, booking a room for herself in the Hotel Vancouver for a month's rest. By July she was meeting for long afternoons with Chief Joe Capilano, whom she had met previously in London, England. Her book *The Legends of Vancouver* would be based on these meetings with the chief, who was already dying of tuberculosis. Eventually she found herself an apartment within walking distance of Stanley Park, her first permanent residence in seventeen years. There she served tea, entertained her many friends, and wrote for various magazines.

Those same friends could not help but notice the dark circles under her eyes and dramatic weight loss. For some time, she had been aware of a lump in her breast. Under duress she agreed to visit a twenty-six-year-old doctor, the one physician in Vancouver experienced with the treatment of cancer. The doctor found the tumor inoperable. Typically, Johnson demanded the news be kept secret and settled down to finish her writing. In March 1910 her good friend Chief Joe Capilano died. At the funeral, a young man standing next to her heard Pauline Johnson whisper to herself, "I'm coming, I'm coming ..."

When the shooting pains in her arm prevented her from writing, she lay on her couch and dictated. Except for the occasional informal talk, which she gave from a sitting position, the days of her wild, heart-pounding recitations were over. In June 1911 she wrote a letter to "My dear good Yeigh-man," thanking the generosity of her friends at a time when "I am too ill to wield a pen and earn my own Muck a Muck."

In the time of her greatest need she was not alone. The careful attentiveness she paid to her friendships, to the making of new friends, to keeping them, the endless gracious notes of thank-you, the efforts to stay in touch were all rewarded during those painful days when her life was being consumed. Men trudged dirty boots across her sick room, told bawdy stories, and made her laugh. Women held her while she wept with pain. Perhaps the critic Theodore Watts-Dunton had it right when he said that with Pauline Johnson "gratitude ... was not a sentiment merely ... but a veritable passion."

In a period of brief remission, she worked energetically on *Flint and Feather*, a compilation of her prose and poems. In mid August of 1912, the pains returned. In September, the Duke of Connaught, Canada's governor general, paid a visit to her hospital room. His assistance allowed her to fulfil a dying wish: to be buried in Stanley Park. Described as "little more than a skeleton," she clung to life long enough to effect a reconciliation with her estranged sister Eva, and died March 7, 1913. The flags of Vancouver flew at half mast.

History has judged the work of E. Pauline Johnson to be of little value. Even by the 1930s, the Canadian literary establishment had relegated her to a type of sentimental curiosity piece: "a pretty legend ... a very genteel lady in a bustle who had nice thoughts." Nonetheless, her biography has been written at least five times, and will be written again. As readers we are now fully sensitive to the unsavoury side of the "Indian Poetess" phenomenon. She was, after all, born on the richest, most Europeanized Indian reserve in Canada, never played with Mohawk children, never learned a Native language, or had, until the end, a Native friend. In order to appear a convincing "Indian" on stage, she was forced to order an Indian outfit from the Hudson's Bay Company in Winnipeg — the first time in her life she had ever worn Native garments. In an attempt to bolster her career, she wooed Canada's most powerful racist, Duncan Campbell Scott. Constantly broke, she wheeled and dealt her Indian "curios" with the relish of a pawnbroker. "A Hiawatha League (wampum belt)" was, she said, worth $1600, "but I would accept much less for it." These irreplaceable artifacts she offered to any buyer she could find. Tragically she became a publicity doll for the same Canadian nationalism that was tearing Native children from their families and forcing them into the horrors of the residential school. She was dimly aware of it. "I am slave to money," she wrote, "doll of the people." When she sobs melodramatically to Ernest Thompson Seton, "never let anyone call me a *white woman*," it is difficult not to see her as a pathetic figure.

In spite of all of this, Johnson achieved a level of popularity that no Canadian writer will ever reach again. Her poem "The Song My Paddle Sings" is perhaps the most famous poem ever written on Canadian soil. Memorized by three generations of Canadians, there are women today who can still recite its clear musical lines. In her own lifetime and for several decades after, there was barely a schoolchild in Canada who did not know the name of her pony (Marengo) the name of her canoe (*Wildcat*) or the name of the house where she grew up (Chiefswood). Her long essay "My Mother" equals anything published on this subject, and "A Strong Race Opinion on the Indian Girl in Modern Fiction," is a thoughtful rebuke of racial stereotypes in literature and tackles the thorny issues of "voice appropriation" eighty years before the term had even been coined.

Today, in an age of intense gender analysis, what is most noticeable about her writing is her instinctive and unstoppable womanization of the world. In a landscape almost universally depicted as male, everything has become female; the cities, the mountains, even the houses of Vancouver are "sisterly houses." A poet, she says, "is like a mother." There are no tigers in Johnson's work, only "she-tigers" and "she-panthers." It is sometimes astonishing to feel how alive, how active this is in her writing. Closely allied to this is the struggle of the sexes. This struggle does not take place against each other, but together and is based on love instead of rancor. It is a struggle in which worldly righteousness is found incarnate in the woman who, in turn, finds her most supreme expression in "The Mother ... the queen mother" who possesses the "Mother Heart." Only slightly less exalted is "the wife" followed by "the girl child." In all three stages, her love of a man or boy, and particularly her own infant, is explosive. She will allow herself to be killed for this love, and she will kill herself, and others if necessary.

For Johnson, the highest plane a person can reach is the memory of his or her mother's teaching and love. Protected by this love, the possessor of it "never grows old, never grows weary, never grows commonplace." The men, women, and children in her world live and die in love. The greater the love, the greater the tragedy of death, and the greater likelihood of it happening. This battle of love fights forever in her prose and poetry; it leads to tragedy and happiness, it leads to the great union of the redskin and paleface civilizations.

In this extraordinary story she wrapped an entire continent. From Brantford to Vancouver, everything is born of a mother's love. From Rainy River to Lillooet Falls, a mother's love forges the beauty and the grandeur of northern people: "A thousand mother lights gleamed from her eyes, a thousand measures of mother love stormed at her heart."

In the case of an Indian woman, this love is visible, it can actually be seen, appearing "thin, fine, silvery as a cobweb." This Mother Woman and her love becomes the supreme achievement of the human race, even more supreme when the mother woman happens to be an Indian, and most supreme of all, when the Indian is Mohawk.

Her critics allowed none of this. Instead they focused on her predictable British patriotism and the patently commercial elements to her writing. The standard critical line on Pauline Johnson is that of a young talent destroyed by a career of travel and stage recitations. Without exception we are informed that "her constant touring was a handicap to the development of her genius." In one of the most condescending remarks imaginable, a distant relative, sister of American novelist W.D. Howells wrote of her; "The poor thing has a hard time of it ... she and a young Californian [sic] give a third rate show in the small towns about the country, and don't do much for Art nor for themselves." Constant touring we are told, "deadened her creative spirit," and "diverted her from the path of pure poetry."

Today it seems obvious that the fullest expression of Pauline Johnson's achievement is to be found in the astonishing distances she covered. She saw more of her country than perhaps any man or woman alive. She crossed the Rocky Mountains nineteen times; she crossed the Atlantic Ocean six times. She once stood on an Edmonton street corner and watched a dog train bring in six thousand dollars' worth of mink pelts. In Ontario, she gave a benefit recital to purchase a wooden leg for a police officer. In Nova Scotia, she watched her own advertising flyers eaten off telephone poles by goats. She performed from Steinway Hall, London, England, to Jerry Boyer's saloon at High River. She rode on trains that wrecked, sailed on ships that sank, and slept in hotels that burned down on her. She crossed the prairies countless times in minus-forty-degree weather, and she loved every minute of it. It is said that there is not a single town or settlement in Canada that she did not visit. At Girard, British Columbia, she was the only woman in town. She gave impromptu recitals while waiting for a train, sending a boy out through the streets of the settlement ringing a bell, shouting, "Pauline Johnson! Pauline Johnson! Concert tonight!" In Bakerville, heading south to Soda Creek, she performed in a barn. Her dressing room was an oat bin with a Hudson's Bay Company blanket strung across it so the audience couldn't see her undress. At Kuskanook she performed on a billiard table that she mounted from a soap box. Her London-made evening gown still had the oats clinging to it while she cried out:

> "I am Ojistoh, I love you, love you
> love you as my life."
> And buried in his back his scalping knife.

Men walked for miles from the mines and the bush, carrying their own planks to sit on, to pay a day's wage to see her and to listen. At one of these events, her coach driver (she nicknamed him "Cariboo Billy") doubled as doorman and ticket-taker and erected a sign that read WHITES A DOLLAR — INDIANS FIFTY CENTS. One man objected on the grounds that he was half white and half Indian. "Fine," roared the driver. "Seventy-five cents!" The customer bought his ticket, completely satisfied. The recital was followed by a party in which Johnson danced until dawn, climbed back into the stage coach, and set off for the next settlement, and the next performance.

This is what she saw: the frontier where human society flew by the seat of its pants, and the rules were made up as the game got played. She was a woman who chased this frontier even as it vanished in front of her, knowing that it was transitory, that it would be soon gone forever. She was there witnessing the death of pioneer Canada, and when Caribou Billy died in 1908, she consoled herself by noting that "he had made his exit in the very scene that saw the romance of the play on the wane —"

A fitting observation from the woman who played the lead role.

7

J.R. Booth:
The Fire King

On some maps the town is called Killaloe Station, since that's what it was at one time: a station through which goods were carried, mostly timber from Algonquin Park, great white pines that decked the battleships of the British Navy, and built the window frames of Europe. Corundum went out, and quartz, and the bones of buffalo, piled up for years on western railway sidings, bleached by sun, and shipped east to fertilize an Ottawa gardening craze.

It is rumoured that the spring water at Killaloe can keep a person alive for a hundred years, but this has not translated into any general activity. There are no pines or buffalo bones moving through anymore. The Chip Wagon is shut for the season, and a sturdy blond-haired women sells corn from the back of her pickup truck out by the old rail bed. The train station is gone, as are the tracks, taken up in the 1980s by the great-grandsons of the men hired to lay them down a century before. They worked for J.R. Booth, the lumber baron. People called him King of the Ottawa Valley. A great man, they said. "A man whose depth of vision set him apart from other men," wrote the newspapers.

* * *

John Randolphus Booth was born in 1827 of obscure parentage at Shefford County, Quebec, one of five children. As a young man, he moved to Vermont where he worked as a carpenter and built bridges for the railway. Later he returned to the Ottawa Valley and managed a sawmill. After work, he and his wife split shingles and sold them. He established a machine shop that burned to the ground immediately, the first of many fires that scorched their way through his life.

In 1858, J.R. Booth entered history when he underbid all tenders and won the contract to supply lumber and deal boards to build the country's first Parliament Buildings. In taking out the timbers for this project, Booth became the first timberman to use horses in the bush. Until then, exclusively oxen had been employed. In 1862, he secured a fortune by purchasing 250 square miles of timber rights on the Madawaska River. Booth sold it at auction. With a prescient knowledge of what the value would prove to be, he told his cousin, "The pine stands like grass. Buy at any cost."

Over the next few years, the King established a fiefdom of piling yards and sawmills that extended into the United States. By the 1880s, his steamboats floated logs to market, his railway spurs got to trees the rivermen could no longer reach. The forest of eastern Canada disappeared before him like a tide. By the end of the eighties, his network of lumber shanties was connected — by telephone.

In 1892, J.R. Booth paid $24,000 to get a Conservative elected in south Renfrew County. He was informed it would cost fifty thousand dollars for a Conservative, but, like everything else, he found a way to do things cheaper. He built the largest lumber mill in the world in Ottawa, turning out a million board feet a shift and producing the world's largest piles of sawdust — which he dumped into the Ottawa River. When city officials insisted he stop, Booth threatened to move his operations elsewhere. In 1893, the mill burned to the ground. It was the first of four major fires to strike it.

By the early nineties, he'd built a railway from Ottawa to Parry Sound, the largest privately owned railway in the world. Somehow he managed to run it directly through Algonquin Park, which had just been established and explicitly forbade the passage of railways. This line, the OAPS, was known locally as "Only Abuse and Poor Salary." The Ottawa, Arnprior, Parry Sound Railway gave Booth year-round access to the trees of the eastern pinery, cut straight through the wilderness of Ontario, and aggregated five hundred miles through almost unpopulated land. The last primeval pines of the Ontario forest travelled east on his line.

To save money, Booth put his western railway terminus not at Parry Sound, but on a nearby Indian reservation. The Indians of Parry Island Reservation No. 16 were unanimous in opposition to a railway terminal. They sent their objections in two separate letters to the head of the Department of Indian Affairs, Hayter Reed. Reed turned the land over to J.R. Booth, confident it would be "in the best interest of the Indians themselves."

Under pressure from the Department, more than three hundred acres of land were surrendered to J.R. Booth on the condition he build a bridge for pedestrian use, that safety fences be constructed, and that no liquor be sold. The fences were never built, the pedestrian bridge took sixty years, bootlegging began immediately, and railway dynamiting forced the closure of the only Indian school on the island.

A photograph of John Randolphus Booth now hangs in the Barry's Bay funeral parlour and shows an old man, standing with his two sons, also elderly, in front of the last shipment of squared timber to leave Algonquin Park. The year is 1925 and the King is tapping his stick on one of the enormous squared trunks, which will never be seen again. A white beard fringes a granite face, making him look like a cruel king, or at least a humourless one.

At one time the government granted him seven thousand square miles, the largest timber limit in the world. We know from the old stories that one day while out inspecting it, he got lost. Perhaps he was counting trees, translating diameter inches into cubic feet of board. He was counting money. As the trees went, the price of pine escalated at an astonishing rate. In 1857, to finance his wedding, a man sold his timber rights for $250. Thirty years later the timber was valued at $600,000.

Somewhere, in the midst all that money, J.R. Booth got lost. He turned one way but that way was the way he just turned from. He turned again. A pine branch scratched his forehead and left a line of blood. Then he remembered that he was not a commoner, he was King. For that reason he did not succumb to the fear that sends a lesser man running through the forest. Mr. Booth sat down. "I am King," he reasoned. "My people will look for me." Between the mills and the timberfields, two thousand men worked for him.

At dusk two men appeared between the trees.

"Mr. Booth? We're ready to go now, sir."

They pretended Mr. Booth was never lost.

"Let's go then," said the old man, and lifted himself off the black trunk.

In his long career he handpicked and bankrolled the mayor of Ottawa and gave political advice to Sir John A. Macdonald. When schools got in the way of his railway, he shut them down.

When those schools asked to be compensated, he threatened to stop hiring local men. He kept his legal teams in court defending him against charges that his mills were burning down the forests of Algonquin Park. His mills *were* burning down the forests of Algonquin Park.

He was a humourless, cheap, unforgiving, ruthless man who never gave money to charity, refused to serve fresh meat to his workers, and sometimes, in a moment of sleeplessness, tormented by the heat and mosquitoes, it is not impossible that he saw stumps like the broken teeth of a fighter, spreading as far as North Bay and beyond. To the east those same white stumps. For ten thousand years the largest covering of tall pine on earth stood here, waving in the wind. In his lifetime he made it disappear. Even when he had more money than it was possible to count and his mansions scattered across eastern Ontario like acorn seeds, he kept taking the trees.

A future prime minister would, for some reason, call him "a great man," and "one of the fathers of Canada." But still, the vision of those stumps, some twelve feet around, spread to the horizon and beyond. Every year he left a million stumps behind. He was seventy-eight years old and had many more years to live. This is what he had done, and on rare moments at night, the fear entered his room.

By the turn of the century, J.R. Booth owned more timberland than anyone else in Canada. His sawmill at Ottawa was the largest in the world. But he suffered. In 1848 his two-year-old had daughter died of scarlet fever. In 1866, he lost his six-year-old daughter. Three years later, his fifteen-month-old son, Frank, passed away. In 1886, his wife Rosalinda Cooke, age fifty-seven, died of pneumonia. His twenty-three-year-old daughter died of pulmonory tuberculosis in 1899. His own mother had died when she was twenty-nine.

He outlived five of his eight children, and through these tragedies the forest kept receding and the fires kept burning. In 1893,
Booth's lathe mill in Ottawa burned to the ground. An arsonist
set his main mill on fire. A year later, two fires devastated his
lumberyard in Vermont. In 1896, a forest fire raged through his
timber holdings near Eganville, Ontario, leaving clouds of smoke
too dense for trains to penetrate. In 1900, the Great Hull-Ottawa
Fire swept out of Hull, Quebec, leapt the Ottawa River, and razed
half the city. He lost a mansion, six stables, twenty tenements,
fifty million board feet of lumber, and eight horses. A year later,
a fire ripped through his pineries of Kippewa and Témiscaming.
In 1903, ten million board feet of lumber burst into flames at his
Wellington and Broad Street lumber yards. The SS *Booth*, the
largest ship to ply the waterways of Lake Nipissing, burnt to the
waterline, and sank. In 1913, five separate fires burnt through
his Ottawa mills in a single month. His sulphite mill burst into
flames. In the last year of his life, a forest fire ravaged his four
thousand hectares on the Madawaka River.

Ninety years ago, J.R. Booth's timber trains rode back and forth
across this valley, six, seven times a day, every day for forty years,
until the trees were gone. And when the last tree was gone, J.R.
Booth lay down and died. He was ninety-nine years old, but the
flames were not finished. At his request, the letters, diary notes,
receipts, and documents accumulated during his long life, were
placed in a drum and set on fire; an extraordinary act, a strange
nose-thumbing at history, perhaps a frightened gesture by a man
who had a great deal to hide.

Even with his death, the fires were not done with him. On
January 1, 1956, a fire broke out on the third floor of a great
Ottawa baronial mansion that J.R. Booth had bequeathed to

his son, Fred. It was in this house that the Prince of Demark renounced his rights to the throne by marrying Fred Booth's daughter, Lois Frances, a commoner. It was from this building that Igor Gouzenko removed sensitive documents prior to his defection in 1945 — the building had been expropriated by the Canadian government and given to the Soviets three years earlier.

Despite a shouting match with the mayor of Ottawa, Soviet staff refused to allow the fire department onto the grounds and the great former Booth mansion was gutted by flames.

8

James McIntyre:
The Cheese Poet

The man universally celebrated as Canada's worst poet was born in Forres, Scotland, in 1828, and immigrated to Upper Canada thirteen years later. Not much is known of his early years in the New World, and the poet himself shed little light on the subject when he penned the less than immortal couplet

> The first winter which I did spend
> In Canada was with a friend

It is known that in the late 1840s, James McIntyre apprenticed in St. Catharines, Ontario, as a builder of furniture and eventually an undertaker (those two professions were often sensibly filled by the same person). Of that town he would leave behind another less than spectacular couplet:

> St. Catharines famed for mineral waters
> And for the beauty of her daughters

From St. Catharines he moved to Ingersoll, Ontario, the emerging heartland of the Canada's dairy industry, and a town founded, some say, by Laura Secord's father. It was also the town where, in 1858, ten thousand curious folk flocked to observe the alligator-like monster that lurked in the village pond. The beast turned out to be a semi-submerged stuffed cow.

In Ingersoll, James McIntyre practised and perfected his versifications, leading a later mayor of Ingersoll to compare him to the famously terrible Scottish poet, William McGonagall, whose club-footed verses actually got him run out of town. "He was every bit as bad as McGonagall," boasted the mayor, "and a lot less talented." The once-celebrated American poet Joachim Miller, in a backhanded compliment that McIntyre himself delighted in quoting, said of him that he "did wise in singing of useful themes." Even the writer of McIntyre's lengthy and glowing obituary that appeared in 1906 felt compelled to remind the reader, once again, that James McIntyre's verse "was probably not of the highest literary standard." The Toronto *Globe* obituary thought it prudent to not mention his poetry at all. A half-century ago, *Maclean's* magazine described him as "our best bad poet," and currently at least one website describes him as "a writer of crap poetry."

Today it is that clear that what has caused a century and a half of critics to hold their collective noses over his verse, was James McIntyre's decision to write poems about a subject on which, according to G.K. Chesteron, poets have remained mysteriously silent — cheese. The decision to write almost exclusively about cheese, Canadian cheddar in particular, has earned MacIntyre such titles as The Chaucer of Cheese, or simply The Cheese Poet, and has virtually guaranteed him a small, if extremely modest slice of literary recognition.

Having arrived in Ingersoll, Ontario, in 1854, MacIntyre quickly established himself as a first-rate maker of cabinets, pianos, and coffins ("The people all say and declare that it is true/The best furniture is made by McIntyre's glue) and a third-rate writer of poems. Fortunately, for the sake of his poetry, he found himself living in the emerging heartland of the Canada's dairy industry, a region eager to promote its cheese-making expertise. This was done, in particular, by the production of single, enormous attention-getting cheese, a 7,300-pound circle immediately christened "The Mammoth Cheese." It was on this subject that McIntyre was to write his most beloved and best known poem, "Ode on the Mammoth Cheese," which, outside of John McCrae's "In Flanders Fields" include what are perhaps the most frequently reprinted lines in all of Canadian poetry:

> We have seen thee queen of cheese
> Lying quietly at your ease
> Gently fanned by evening breeze

It took twelve horses to haul the massive cheddar to the Saratoga, New York, state fair where it proved too much for the makeshift stage and crashed through it. While not all sources agree on this point, it seems more likely to be true than a note posted on the *Oxford Curd Gird* website, which insists that the Mammoth Cheese of McIntyre's poem scalded twenty people during the Great Cheethamshire Fondue disaster of 1867.

Despite the light-hearted manner in which James McIntyre has come to be viewed, his own life was far from trouble-free. His wife and son both died within in a year of one another. An ill-advised partnership led to bankruptcy and in the spring of 1891, high waters washed away his business. In a telegram, his daughter Kate Ruttan wrote: COFFINS CASKETS CARD TABLES PIANOS PIANOLOS BEDS BUNK ETC SAILED DOWN RIVER THAMES. She would say of her father at this time that "he couldn't pay for a sitting hen." She also neatly described him as "forty years a Free Mason and fifty years an Oddfellow."

Kate Ruttan was herself one of those tantalizing figures who inhabit the shadowy recesses of local history and refuse to come out into the open. In her eccentric life as a schoolteacher, she was apparently dismissed, more than once, for her relaxed teaching methods. After a series of jobs, which included peddling Billy Sunday's evangelical tracts door to door, and, more dubiously, "firing for a freight train," she settled in as postmistress with the assignment of meeting the night train to collect the mail sacks. She also doubled as a weekly columnist for the *Fort Frances Times,* for which she wrote under the name Charming Kitty. A true eccentric, her face was rarely, if ever, seen in public, as she went about town dressed in a thick veil. Her marital status was complex, and involved at least two husbands, neither of whom she seemed to live with or ever mention. Although her domestic skills were said to be lacklustre at best, her home was known locally as The Reading Room, or the Ruttan Reading Room, and became the Rainy River equivalent of a literary salon. Kate was herself no slouch when it came to the art of bad poetry. Her own verse reached such memorable heights as,

> Billy Boy and Bobby Martin
> Were speedy runners sure and sartin

She penned what is surely one the world's most peculiar advertisements for the funeral industry when she wrote these lines in praise of her father's business:

> An undertaker bold
> who can't be undersold …
> and incomplete his verses
> did we forget his hearses?

She suggests later in the poem that to be embalmed by James MacIntyre entitled the customer to a certain perk, a free copy of her father's poems:

> His book he'll give you gratis
> Filled with divine afflatus

In attempt to convince the recalcitrant local fiddler Walter McFayden to perform more often, she dipped deep into her Scottish heritage to entice him with the following: "Wull ye no have a hope very Friday nicht, Walter and give the wee winsome thing a chance till ease their chilblains?"

She was the author of one book, *Rhymes Both Right and Wrong of Rainy River*, a collection of what critics have called "execrable" poems, published two year before her death. This small book, now a collector's item, was sold door to door by Kate in the final few years before she died of food poisoning.

Together, James and Kate formed a sort of Golden Age in Canadian bad poetry, unmatched perhaps until the 1950s when the Newfoundland barrister R.A. Parsons deemed fit to clank his rhymes in public:

> For thou art but a little house, of roof
> That lets a stove pipe through, still weather proof

Unfortunately the golden badness of R.A. Parsons' verse is sometimes fatally compromised by the writer's ambition to be good poet. Neither James McIntyre nor his daughter suffered from this. It seems they both knew exactly how bad their poetry was and were engaging in some calculated and subversive fun by imitating the not-very-lofty example of celebrated second-rate poets everywhere. McIntyre himself was a formidable Shakespeare scholar and a much called-upon public speaker in Ingersoll. He seemed quite content to write verse that celebrated and promoted the industrial products of the region where he lived. Nor, in fairness, was his subject matter limited entirely to cheese. The death of Shelley, for example, inspired four lines that would have put a grin on even T.S. Eliot's grey face:

> We have scarcely time to tell thee
>> Of the strange and gifted Shelley
> Kind-hearted man but ill-fated
> So youthful, drowned and cremated.

The crushing dreadfulness of these rhymes is arguably beyond the reach of a great many poets, and so is the wit. McIntyre also versified freely about the potato bug, the typewriter (no thank you), and electric light. He was not afraid to take on departed statesmen such as Joseph Howe:

> Joseph Howe, none stood higher than thou
> Though wert a man with lofty brow

He once wrote a poem about Lord Stratchcona's horse, and his 1927 biographer notes that, "Whenever cows come on the scene…the poet grows particularly tender." Perhaps he was referring to these lines

...contented with their fate
the gentle cows do ruminate

Poultry was not beyond his reach either, as the following lines demonstrate:

And in Ontario the hen
is worthy of the Poet's pen

Somewhere in that subversive couplet lies the ingenious McIntyre method that was to be repeated over and over again: the grandiose, pompous diction from which the air is rapidly escaping. It starts fine enough, but by the time the end is reached, the rhythm and the meaning have collided in a crashing tangle of cliché, expectation, and a final rhyme that is always too crushingly exact, and reveals the poet to be the smallest of small-town rubes.

Today the legacy of Canada's worst versifier lives on rather more noisily in the poetry slam and the open-mic stage where earnest men and women show an appalling inability to do what James MacIntyre and his daughter did so well: laugh at themselves. It also lives on in Ingersoll, Ontario, where, since 1997, the local library has sponsored the James McIntyre Poetry Contest for area residents. Every year aspiring bad poets submits such gems as:

Just say to me, "Please,"
And I'll give you some cheese.

And the slightly more ambitious:

The railroads in Ingersoll are busy,
sometimes they make me dizzy

It is doubtful though, that anyone will surpass the modesty and the sheer technical tedium of the master himself when he dwells on his chosen theme:

And let us all with songs and glees
Invoke success into the cheese.

9

Tom Longboat:
Who Do You Think I Am?

The story goes that somewhere in France during the Great War, a British general was being led to the front by a dispatch runner. Struggling to keep up, the general grew irritated with the pace set by the runner and ordered him to slow down. "For God's sake," he complained. "Who do you think I am? Tom Longboat?"

The dispatch runner, a tall, slender fellow, slowed and answered truthfully, "No sir. That's me."

This story, apocryphal or not, demonstrates the enormous fame of a young Onondagan from southern Ontario who, for a brief moment, was one of the most celebrated men alive. Over the course of his career, millions of people assembled to watch him. When his glory faded he became what the newspapers called "the original dummy ... a lazy ... stall fed ... Injun" and a "stubborn," once-talented "Redskin" who ended his days a penniless alcoholic. Or so the papers would have us believe.

Thomas Charles Longboat was born on the Six Nations Reserve, seven miles outside of Caledonia, Ontario, on June 4, 1886. The second of three children, his father died when he was five. His mother, according to the *Toronto Telegram* possessed "Indian hair," "small shrewd eyes ... Hers is an Indian face," concluded the reporter, adding, with some surprise, that her granddaughter was playing with a "rag dolly, just like her white sisters" might do.

Born a member of the Wolf Clan and raised in the Longhouse religion, the infant Tom Longboat was christened *Cogwagee*. In English the name translates as "Everything" and hints at the difficulties reporters would face in a fifty-year struggle to define him.

As a young boy he was required to attend the Mohawk Institute, an Anglican residential school. He escaped — significantly — by running away. By twelve he was a farm labourer. It is said he developed his "running legs" while chasing cows in the fields and that he once ran forty miles from Hamilton, Ontario, to Brantford, arriving home before his mother who had left hours earlier — in a wagon. At nineteen he ran the annual Victoria Day race at Caledonia and placed second, catching the eye of Native runner Bill Davis. Davis, a Mohawk, had placed second in the 1901 Boston Marathon behind fellow Canadian Jack Cafferty — a celebrated race joined, for several miles, by a spooked horse. It was Davis who provided Longboat with his first high-calibre coaching. In 1906 he entered the Hamilton Herald race where, in a field of forty, including tested professionals, odds against Longboat went as high as a hundred to one. During the race, he took a wrong turn and ran seventy-five yards before someone corrected him. He won by nearly four minutes. At first, race officials believed their watches had malfunctioned. According to the *Hamilton Herald*, a twenty-year-old Tom Longboat left his nearest competitor "as if he had been standing still."

* * *

In becoming a runner, this young Onondagan was engaging in a significant, if loosely understood, aspect of early Native civilization. Running is said to bring myths to life and create a link between runners and the universe. It is also useful in times of war. When Cortez touched shore in 1519, within twenty-four hours runners had provided descriptions of his ships, men, and weapons to Montezuma, three hundred miles away. Runners of messages in the Iroquois Confederacy (Longboat was in this tradition) carried news from the Atlantic seaboard to the Niagara Frontier, running day and night, navigating by stars. The Hopi Indian, Louis Tewanima — a rival of Longboat who, at the age of eighty, walked twenty miles a day herding sheep, and at ninety died by falling off a mountain — was said to have routinely run one hundred and twenty miles barefoot, "just to watch the trains pass." Anthropologists believe the strength invested in a Mesquakie ceremonial runner included not only "the holy power of speed," but the power to be invisible. And, in this century, there are reports of a Native runner from southern California who once left Cottonwood Island in Nevada at sunrise, only to arrive at Fort Yuma at the exact same moment that he left.

It was out of this remarkable and mysterious tradition that Tom Longboat emerged. With several more races under his belt, all victories, the twenty-year-old was ready to compete against the best marathoners in North America. In 1907, in what would be perhaps the most celebrated sports event of all time, Tom Longboat, under the banner of the West Toronto YMCA, entered the Boston Marathon. Almost unbelievably, his fame as a runner had spread through the intense world of long-distance running — a world where North American Natives were well represented and often excelled. On the basis of his Ontario races, he had become, overnight, a legend. Newspapers were already calling him "the greatest distance runner the world has ever seen." Suddenly this previously unknown young man was now the odds-on favourite to win. When Longboat shunned pre-race interviews, local newspapers fabricated them and rushed them into print. Unable to get a photograph, they substituted a picture of a Native football player and ran that instead.

On the morning of April 19, 1907, an estimated one hundred thousand people lined up to watch the eighth running of the Boston Marathon. The route spanned twenty-five miles, the course was hilly, and the temperature was cool. At the sound of a pistol shot, 124 runners surged forward. Several miles in at Farmingham, a freight train intersected the race at a street crossing. Ten runners, including Longboat, made it through; the rest were forced to wait more than a minute while the train cleared. (The early years of distance-running were prone to such events; in an Ontario race, a horse-drawn wagon toppled over on Longboat, who crawled out from beneath it and went on to win.) Out in the hills of Boston where the race would end, a snow squall struck. Having already run twenty-four miles, Longboat sprinted the final mile, uphill, into slanting snow, in an astonishing four minutes and forty-six seconds, smashing the course record, set by Canadian Jack Cafferty, by a full five minutes. His nearest competitor lagged a full mile behind. It is said Longboat had already picked up his trophy and was eating dinner as fellow racers crossed the line. A Boston headline stated: "Hills Held No Terror for Redskin."

Tom Longboat returned to Toronto and to a triumph that is difficult to imagine today. Two hundred thousand people lined the streets and bands played. "Young women gazed at [him] in rapture." Longboat, with a Union Jack draped around his shoulders, was placed in an open car and driven through the city at the head of a torchlit parade. People lit brooms on fire and waved them through the air. Traffic came to a standstill. Streetcar drivers, unable to move, handed out unpunched transfers, having no idea when the streets might clear. Longboat, looking uncomfortable beneath the crush of adoration, was given a gold medal and the keys to the city. "The British Empire is proud of you," boomed the mayor, and announced a five-hundred-dollar gift to go to the runner's education.

It is not clear if the mayor intended to honour this promise. The funds are paternalistically tied to the assumption that the Native is in need of improvement. Longboat responded in a touching letter, almost disarming in its humility.

> R.T. Coady, Esq.,
> City Treasurer.
> Dear Sir:
> I understand you have collected a fund for my education. I do not want to accept it that way, as I am in business now and am getting enough education every day, and I am daily trying to improve myself in every way.
>
> Could you request the city to pay this money over to build a house for my mother on the Onondaga Reserve. The money could be spent by the Trustees, my mother to have the house for life and after her death it to go to me. I am told legislation will have to be obtained to sanction this.
>
> Have to thank all who so kindly contributed, and the citizens of Toronto generally for helping me in every way while here
> Kindly do what you can for me as above, and oblige.
> Yours truly,
> Thomas Longboat.

Nothing came of the request.

* * *

Even in the most celebrated moment of Tom Longboat's career, newspaper writers could not conceal their discomfort with him. To the racial assumptions they had grown up with, Longboat posed a perplexing challenge. A member of a supposedly "pathetic" and vanishing race, a poorly educated, barely literate "Injun," he was also, tall, handsome, and now extremely famous. He also appeared in the company of attractive women, not all of them Native. The tension they felt is obvious in what they wrote: "It is hoped that Longboat's success will not develop obstinacy on his part, and that he will continue to be manageable," cautioned the *Toronto Star*.

"Obstinate" and "unmanageable," are terms that better describe horses and are symptomatic of the newspapers depiction of Tom Longboat as an animal, often a horse in need of breaking. In print he became a "lanky, raw-boned, headstrong Redskin" who did not run, but "galloped." Faced with a compliment, he "would smile as wide as a hippo and gurgle his thanks." Sportswriter Lou Marsh described the young Onondagan "smiling like a coon in a watermelon patch." Marsh, a popular *Toronto Star* sports columnist who would carry on a bizarre and nasty campaign against Longboat, confidently described him to his readers as "the original dummy." "Wiley ... unreliable ... as hard to train as a leopard."

The difficulty writers experienced trying to pinpoint the man is suggested in the quantity of nicknames they stuck on him. He was tagged the Bronze Cyclone, the Racing Redskin, the Wonderful Redskin, Tireless Tom, Big Chief, Heap Big Chief, the Great Indian, even the Irish Indian. This confusion of titles did not so much describe a man named Tom Longboat, but the tentative and confused efforts of white newspapermen to integrate a world famous Canadian Indian into the racial hierarchies of the time.

A cruel, but revealing comment came from a *Toronto Star* writer who, after Longboat's triumph at Boston, wrote "His trainers are to be congratulated … for having such a docile pupil."

If Longboat was to gain the respect of the media, it would not be by proving himself the greatest runner in the world, which he would soon do, but by becoming "docile" and "manageable." This would prove more difficult.

On the heels of his Boston victory, a twenty-one-year-old Tom Longboat was evicted from his YMCA lodgings for reasons described alternately as "breaking curfew," smoking, drinking a bottle of beer, or being in the company of women. His management was taken over by Tom Flanagan, director of the Irish Canadian Athletic Club, a flamboyant Toronto sports promoter. Longboat had initiated contact with a brief note to the man. The letter, all fourteen words, typifies the reserve that reporters found so maddening in him: "Dear Sir — I want to join the Irish Canadian Club. Enclosed find a dollar."

Perhaps no one personified the seedy, free-wheeling world of sports promotion as did Longboat's new manager. "A nattily dressed blade of twenty-eight," he made this revealing comment about the British marathoner Alfred Shrubb: "First of all, I apologize to Alfred Shrubb for hitting him. I'm not a blackguard." He once raced Longboat twelve miles against a horse named Sam McBee. Longboat won after Flanagan positioned himself in front of a bridge and insisted to a police constable that he enforce the posted by-law for bridges: "Riders Walk Your Horse." The subterfuge proved unecessary—the horse eventually dropped dead. Flanagan's first concern was preserving the delicate condition of Longboat's amateur status so that he might run in the 1908 Olympics. This he did by setting up Tom Longboat with a job in a cigar store: Longboat's Athletic Cigar Store. Confined to stool in a claustrophobic stall, the young Onondagan did not thrive — the popular rumour was that he smoked too many of the cigars himself. Despite controversy and grumbling, in the end, the ruling sports bodies of the day allowed Longboat to compete in the infamous 1908 Olympic Marathon, held in London, England.

The race, today, is remembered for two reasons. Dorando Pietro's excruciating effort in which he collapsed fifty yards from the finish line and was escorted the rest of the way by well-meaning officials — only to be disqualified because of it. That incident resulted in perhaps the most reproduced sports photograph ever taken. The race is also remembered because of Tom Longboat's failure to finish. He either stopped running or collapsed at the nineteenth mile, in second place, and was eventually taken out of the finishing line stadium on a stretcher. Lou Marsh would say he "quit." The race was tainted by the belief that Longboat had been doped; that Flanagan had doped his own runner to ensure his failure, and collect $100,000 in wagers — Longboat being heavily favoured. Others put Longboat's failure down to the heat, which, on that day, was record-breaking.

The race did not sit well with marathon fanatics on both sides of the Atlantic. According to team manager J. Howard Crocker, "Longboat should have won the race. His sudden collapse and the symptoms shown to me indicate that some form of stimulant was used contrary to the rules of the game. Any medical man knowing the facts of the case will assure you that the presence of a drug in an overdose was the cause of the runner's failure."

In a bizarre twist, it has even been suggested that sports writer Lou Marsh, who was following Longboat on a bicycle, may himself have been the person who administered the drugs.

The *Hamilton Spectator* dismissed the whole affair: "Longboat ran a good race [but] could not stand the glare and heat. There was nothing to it ..."

Longboat returned to Canada, announced his retirement, changed his mind, set a new Canadian five-mile record, won his third straight Ward Marathon, and then turned professional. Apparently unsatisfied with Flanagan as a manager, he considered handing his management over to a Mohawk friend from Deseronto, Tom Claus. Sports writers were furious. They eagerly quoted Flanagan to the effect that would-be promoters of Longboat "had sufficiently degraded the Indian by pandering to his weaknesses." A local reverend, John Morrow, waded in "... because the physical and mental make-up of the Indian is so foreign to any other athlete's, and his disposition so hard at times to understand ... I can safely say that no other man ... could have managed Tom Longboat but Flanagan."

Flanagan and his famous client patched up their differences and on November 11, 1908, in his first race as a professional, Longboat defeated a three-man relay team over five miles. A month later he raced Dorando Pietri at Madison Square Garden. Crowds were so thick that Pinkertons had to be called in to reinforce police. Inside, the Garden's air was a dense blue pall of tobacco smoke. Through this barrier the two men would be expected to run twenty-six miles — 260 laps around the arena. Neck and neck for the entire race, Longboat, in a characteristic burst, pulled ahead. Pietri, straining to close the gap, collapsed and was carried unconscious off the track.

Two weeks later Longboat married a Mohawk woman, Lauretta Maracle. The *Globe* wrote, approvingly, that the new bride "does not like to talk of feathers, war paint or other Indian paraphernalia ... if anyone can make a reliable man ... of that elusive human being, it will be his wife." Since her Mohawk name translated in English as "The Leader," cut-line writers could safely state: "Mrs. Longboat will therefore be the Leader of Everything." Nothing could shake their notion that Tom Longboat needed to be led. A photo shows the newlyweds posed with a noticeable and telling distance between them.

Five days after the wedding, Longboat raced Dorando Pietri for a third time. In front of eleven thousand people at the Buffalo Armouries, the two runners clocked a killing time of two hours, twenty-six minutes, and thirty-four seconds over the first fifteen miles. Even Lou Marsh admitted a time like that "is not an exhibition by an extra lively tortoise. It is drilling from the drop of the hat." Sniffing or drinking repeatedly from "a little brown dope bottle," Pietri veered off the course at nineteen miles and collapsed into the arms of his brother. Longboat, bleeding at the knees, walked and staggered the remaining miles and took the race.

At the end of January, still complaining of Longboat's unmanageability, Flanagan sold his contract to a New York sports promoter for two thousand dollars. "He sold me just like a racehorse to make money," Longboat told his wife. Flanagan had been best man at their wedding.

In early February he raced Alfred Shrubb, the world's top-ranking professional. When Shrubb took a ten-lap lead, the Madison Square Garden crowd began booing Longboat. Then, unbelievably, he began his comeback, lapping the Englishman again and again over the last six miles. Tom Longboat, age twenty-three, now at the apex of his marathon career, had defeated every great runner in the world at least once.

He did not know it yet, but the brilliant years of his marathon career had come to an end. The interest, the near mania for distance-running, was already waning. Nonetheless, in Edinburgh in

1912 he set a new world's professional fifteen-mile record of one hour and twenty minutes. Volunteering for the army in 1916, he served four years with the 37th Haldimand Battalion of Rifles. His enlistment papers describe his "trade or calling" as "professional runner," and his "complexion … Dark." In a delicious understatement, his certificate of medical examination declares, "he has the free use of his joints and limbs." During his time in France he stood in harm's way and saw the horror that took place on Vimy Ridge and at Passchendaele. He was twice pronounced dead, a ghostly echo of the uncertainty that clouds his public record.

Discharged in 1919, he returned to Caledonia to discover that his wife, during one of his rumoured deaths, had married another man and taken the furniture. Eventually he married an Onondagan, Martha Silversmith, and had four children with her. In the words of a *Maclean's* article, written eight years after his death, "he took another squaw."

The early twenties were difficult years for Tom Longboat. Out of racing, he moved west to collect on a land grant for his war service. He tried various jobs near Edmonton. Apparently he pawned his racing medals, a sad echo of the American Native runner, Ellison "Tarzan" Brown, who sold his medals to buy groceries and was struck dead by a car following an argument in a tavern. An Edmonton lawyer kept Longboat's medals for a number of years, hoping someone would reclaim them. In the end they were melted down for the gold.

He returned to Toronto in 1922. According to one account he was met at the station by his former manager, Tom Flanagan, who bought him a corned-beef sandwich. That same year he was riding the Queen streetcar to south Riverdale where he earned three dollars a day as an employee of the Dunlop Rubber Company. About that time Lou Marsh wrote: "He started out on corn pone, worked up to cavier and now is tickled to get corned beef." In 1924, Longboat asked the Amateur Athletic Union to reinstate him as an amateur so he could run against the Finnish marathoner Paavo Nurmi. Nothing came of it.

He had found a job, however, which he worked faithfully for twenty years. As an employee of the Street Cleaning department of the City of Toronto, he drove horses, swept leaves, and collected garbage. It is in this detail that journalists finally declared victory. "A rubbish man!" they crowed, "A particularly nice rubbish man ... an Indian rubbish man."

"He worked his way to the bottom," wrote Fergus Cronin in the 1957 *Maclean's* article — a low point in Canadian journalism, and a piece of writing that approaches hate literature. When Grolier's published its 1957 *Encyclopedia Canadiana*, the brief entry on Longboat would be drawn entirely from this diatribe.

In 1930, Longboat, now a forty-five-year-old family man, was again in the news. The November 6 issue of the *Globe and Empire* announced that an enemy of the Six Nations reserve had directed "bad medicine" at Longboat and was killing him with it. Of all the mountains of newsprint written about the man, this piece stands alone for the unexpected respect it shows toward Longboat and traditional Native beliefs. In the interview, Longboat talks freely about Native medicine: "The medicine men can do strange things. If a dog comes into their room they can make themselves into that dog. Or they can be in the bear and then be men again. You can see it on the reserve. They can do anything ... People laugh about that wisdom and learning, but they do not realize that they do not know everything."

This is one of the only indications, in print, that Longboat was capable of speaking anything but guttural monosyllables. The piece also provides an intimate picture of the Longboat household. His wife, the "squaw" of Cronin's article, here is a "slim woman ... soft-spoken and courteous." Even his four children warrant names. Apparently the medicine men were capable of helping Longboat, for his malady disappeared.

The most tragic moment of Longboat's life occurred in 1932. Attending the Canadian National Exhibition with his family, he stopped to give a brief interview with Jane Grey, voice of Princess Mus-Kee-Kee, a radio personality for tonics that Longboat endorsed. She asked him if he would like to say hello to anyone. "He told me he would like to speak to his daughter ... Apparently some playmates heard me say this and rushed to call his daughter to the radio. She raced across the path of a car and was instantly killed ... I think she was about eight years old."

Even here, in this moment of Longboat's anguish, the story strays, and the facts become perversely mangled. He *did* lose a child; it *did* happen following a radio interview at the CNE. That child *was* struck dead by a car while trying to race across the street. But the child was a son. His name was Clifford, he was five years old. For the rest of her life, Martha Longboat kept the CNE pennant she'd bought that day, passing it on to a son prior to her death in 1970. The *Maclean's* article, which remained the definitive piece on Longboat for thirty-five years, entirely omits this tragedy, explaining instead that "Garbageman Longboat was broke at forty."

With the arrival of the Second World War, "Garbageman Longboat" enlisted in the Home Guard. By the end of the war, he had retired from his city job, and was living on the Ohsweken reserve where he was born. There was yet one ghost for him to fight. It took the form of a stranger who, for more than a decade, pretended to be Tom Longboat in order to cadge drinks in taverns. This episode has something haunting about it, as though the lazy, drunken "redskin" the newspapers worked so hard to create, had finally risen from the page, to torment the living man. In 1948, Longboat supplied the *Hamilton Spectator* with a photograph of himself, in an effort to foil what he called that "cheap, two-bit imposter."

Back home, in failing health, he walked, every Market Day, seven miles to Hagersville and seven miles back, refusing all offers of a ride. Many years later, a friend, ninety-six-year-old Frank Montour, recalled those long final walks of Tom Longboat; "He was best in the world," said Montour, "and an Indian besides."

The legend of Tom Longboat has been revised over the years. In 1992, a small book written by former Olympic runner Bruce Kidd placed Longboat squarely within the cultural context of his times and indicated what the man was up against. This book is now the main source on Tom Longboat in high school and public libraries across Canada. Cronin's racist brooding has been confined to the dustbins of microfilm. Through Kidd's efforts, the five hundred dollars promised to Longboat by the Toronto mayor, and never paid, was finally collected. With interest it amounted to ten thousand dollars, issued in 1980 to Longboat's heirs. The new *Canadian Encyclopedia*'s entry on Tom Longboat draws entirely from Kidd's book. Websites, school essays, histories of the Boston Marathon ... all of these writings take as their starting point the racial assumptions that once defined the Longboat story.

Today he is presented not as "the original dummy," but a superb athlete; an Onondagan Indian who strode across the earth faster, farther, and more gloriously than any man alive. He has been called Canada's first professional athlete. He was cheered by millions. His name was pronounced in schools, homes, and churches. It is said children spoke of nothing but him. He received fan mail from Clark Gable, shook hands with royalty, and had a cigar named after him. He served in two world wars for a country in which he could not even vote. He was twice pronounced dead. He set times that left professional timekeepers doubting their watches. He saw his own child struck dead by a car. For twenty years he was mocked in print by a spiteful reporter and when that reporter died, he said graciously "he was one of the finest men I ever met." He negotiated the minefield of the dominant culture and even used it to his advantage. He fled the infamy of the residential school system, and when, at the height of his fame, that same school asked him back to give a speech, Longboat refused, saying privately, "I wouldn't even send my dog to that place." Eventually he took work as a garbage collector to support his family. He lived in good homes in respectable neighbourhoods, he drove a car through the height of the Depression, when many Canadians could not even afford bus fare. At the end, when reporters came running to photograph him in his overalls, collecting garbage, he told them, without shame, "I'm doing alright, just living along."

Tom Longboat died January 9, 1949, at the age of sixty-two. His burial ceremony was conducted in the Onondagan way, and a small V-shaped notch was cut in the the coffin lid so that his spirit might race freely to the next world.

10

Cracked Heads and Bloody Noses:
A Brief History of Lacrosse

In 1667, French explorer and translator, a man who was perhaps entirely mad, stood on a hill near Sault Ste. Marie, watching local tribesmen at play. As far as Nicholas Perrot could determine, the object of the game was to use a webbed stick to hurl a deer-hide ball between two poles planted in the opponents' territory. There were no boundaries, the goal areas were miles apart, the game had been going on for days, and more than two thousand men were involved in the action.

Nearly one hundred years later, in 1763, British soldiers stationed at Fort Michilimackinac in today's Michigan, stood on the ramparts watching the same spirited sport taking place in the fields beyond the fort. When a seemingly errant pass put the ball inside the walls, soldiers opened the gates, only to have the Ojibwe and Sauk players race inside and kill them. This event, one of the bloodiest actions of the Pontiac uprising, and a centrepiece of Major John Richardson's *Wacousta*, etched the sport forever in the North American imagination — a sport that graphically lived up to its Algonkian name, *baggataway*, or *tewaarathon*, "the little brother of war."

To the French, the game was "lacrosse," and had been known as such since the 1630s when Jesuit priest Jean de Brébeuf remarked on the resemblance of the webbed stick to a bishop's crozier, or "crosse." In 1837, a Montreal newspaper referred to the games as "Indian lacrosse," announcing that Natives from the village of Caughnawaga had been invited to Montreal to demonstrate the game. This is the first known mention of lacrosse to appear in print. A decade later, the first known lacrosse match between whites and Natives took place. The *Montreal Courier* noted sadly that the seven "gentlemen" from Montreal "were not a match for the (five) red antagonists."

Whether they were a match for their opponents or not, there is no doubt that the light-skinned newcomers were eager to play the game. It has often been remarked that immigrants bring their sports with them. But in Canada it worked the other way. It is doubtful that new Canadians understood much of the game's origin; how it was handed down from the Creator to the First People to strengthen their medicines, resolve disputes, and prepare young men for battle, or that according to an Ojibway tale, the birds themselves flew south each year to atone for losing a lacrosse match. They understood that the game was fast, rough, required considerable skill, and they could not get enough of it.

By the start of 1867 there were six lacrosse teams in Canada. By the close of the same year, there were eighty. Some matches were played in front of crowds of four thousand spectators. It was stated, wrongly, that the new parliament had proclaimed lacrosse "the national game of Canada." A lacrosse-struck dentist from Montreal, the game's first pioneer, promoter, and author, George Beers, enthusiastically, if prematurely, announced that the newly formed Parliament of Canada had given the game its national status. In fact, Parliament had not yet even convened. An association was formed and coined the slogan: "our country and our game." A song, "The Lacrosse Gallop," was written and danced to. Some eager enthusiasts attempted to play at night by dousing the ball in turpentine and setting it on fire. "Fireball lacrosse," proved a failure since not only the ball, but the netting of the sticks and goals also ignited. Night-time lacrosse was temporarily abandoned, but appeared in a less fiery form in 1879, when, for the first time, the game was played beneath electric lights.

In 1876, two touring lacrosse teams from Canada played a match in front of Queen Victoria at Windsor Castle. It would seem the teams were on their best behaviour, even six-foot-two John Baptiste, known as "King of the Lachine Rapids," who played on the Mohawk side. In her diary, the Queen described the match as "very pretty to watch." She also observed, astutely, that the white team had fourteen players and the Native only thirteen. Canadian lacrosse tours of Europe proved so popular that government agents used the games to distribute flyers, urging immigration to Canada.

The rapid spread of lacrosse in Canada was not duplicated in the United States; at least not immediately. There the game was dubbed "mayhem on the lawn ... a madman's game, so wild is it," wrote the *New York Tribune*. A New York writer saw only "cracked heads, bloody noses, and damaged hands, wrist and elbows." *Harper's Weekly* found the game was "too laborious, too exciting for our more nervous and delicate young Americans." Despite these concerns, the game was being imported into the states by Canadian immigrants, and taking root at the collegiate level where it coexisted uneasily with the game played on United States Indian reservations.

For unknown centuries the game was almost entirely without rules or guidelines. The only firm rule seemed to be that the ball could not be touched by hand. Over the years, due to the efforts of George Beers, a structure was gradually imposed. The number of players still fluctuated and the game was declared over once one of the teams had scored three goals. As a result, a match could last for several minutes or be cancelled due to darkness. To the relief of lacrosse promoters, this changed in 1888 when a time limit was set.

With increased popularity of the game came increased conflict. Was lacrosse a gentleman's sport played to develop grace and character, *British* character? Or was it to be sport of paid professionals (most of whom, as it turned out, were Native)? This acrimonious debate swayed back and forth through all Canadian sports for decades, a high-sounding moral excuse to keep superior Native athletes from showing up their betters. In 1880, the National Lacrosse Association of Canada voted entirely in favour of amateurism, effectively barring Native players from organized competition. Try as they might, however, the Native presence in lacrosse could not be denied. Supposedly amateur teams, eager to recruit the best players they could, found ways of importing "ringers;" Native men who could speak passable French or English. The next step was to acquire an English or French name. These names, quickly cobbled together, were not always entirely, or even slightly convincing: "Tom Sam," is one dubious pseudonym for an English-speaking Native ringer. A handy — perhaps *too* handy — French Canadian name like "Jake Leroux" usually concealed a young man of Iroquois origin.

Despite the bickering, the intrigue, and the segregation, Native vs. non-Native competition did not come to an end. An 1882 match between the famed Shamrocks of Montreal and the Cornwall Island Indians saw Cornwall goaltender Frank Lally clear the ball from his net, hurl it the entire length of the field — *and score!* This feat apparently has never been duplicated and perhaps played no small role in helping Mr. Lally become the mayor of Cornwall.

By 1890, British Columbia had formed its own amateur lacrosse association. By 1900, the amateur vs. professional conflict had subsided considerably and amateurs were playing openly against and alongside professionals. One match in British Columbia drew nineteen thousand spectators. In 1901, Canada's governor general, the Earl of Minto, donated the Minto Cup to be contested at the senior national level. Railway magnate Donald Mann commissioned the Mann Cup, battled for by amateur lacrosse teams across the country. First contested in 1910, the Mann Cup is made of solid gold, and, along with the Minto Cup, is one of the longest-running sporting trophies in the world. On the professional side, some lacrosse players were said to be making more money than baseball player Ty Cobb. The old game of lacrosse, played on low, close-cut pastures by boys with homemade shoulder pads and borrowed sticks, had reached its golden age.

The First World War and the years after proved a dark time for the sport. Hockey and baseball were making inroads, as was the sudden passion for weekend auto-touring. The equipment itself worked against the game, preventing its growth. The lacrosse stick was exclusively the handiwork or Native craftsmen and women, and required a year to be bent and set. The gathering and shaping of the hickory was done by the men, and the thong work on the netted pockets by the women. A coach or player could find it necessary to drive sometimes hundreds of miles to the nearest reservation to purchase sticks. On June 4, 1968, a fire hit the Chisholm stick factory on Cornwall Island, where seventy-five men and women produced fifty thousand sticks each year, nearly 100 percent of the supply contintent-wide. Craftsmen responded by working outdoors next to the charred building and with financial help from the federal and provincial government, enough lacrosse sticks were manufactured for the game to go on.

In 1931 the ancient game of *tewaarathon* was radically transformed by the owners of the Montreal Canadiens hockey team.
Their plan was to bring the game indoors and fill up the hockey
arenas sitting empty during summer months. This new game
was dubbed "box lacrosse," and replaced the outdoor field game
almost overnight. Both Native and non-Native players moved
enthusiastically inside. Traditionalists were appalled, especially
American proponents of the field game. The *Baltimore Sun*
described box lacrosse as a mixture of "boxing, hockey, mayhem,
homicide and intent to kill." But to Canadians, the padded shoulders crashing into boards, nets bulging, and red lights flashing,
struck a chord. A dizzying array of leagues were formed, folded,
and started again. Here the Marvelous Mohawk, Ross Powless,
and later his son Gaylord, came to prominence. Ross Powless, a
member of the Canadian Lacrosse Hall of Fame, played on four
Mann Cup teams and twice won the Tom Longboat Trophy as
outstanding Canadian Indian athlete. He also fathered thirteen
children — eight of them lacrosse players, five of them lacrosse
statisticians. As a prominent Native player, Powless took more
than his share of rough play, with angry fans and opponents calling him everything from "Hatchetman" to "Blanketass."

Powless played into the late sixties, racking up extraordinary
statistics. By the seventies his playing career was over and lacrosse
was undergoing a significant alteration. Engineers had developed
a method of making lacrosse sticks from plastic resins — the old
Iroquois game had entered the age of mass production.

In the 1980s, professional box lacrosse arrived in its latest
incarnation. Backed by televised ads of Roman gladiators and
a voiceovers insisting the game made "Sunday football look
like a cabbage patch picnic," a new league was launched, failed,
launched again, evolving finally, in 1997, into the National
Lacrosse League (NLL). Today, players in this multi-million

dollar cross-border league often display their skills in front of more than fifteen thousand fans a game.

For nearly four hundred years, lacrosse has been a point of contact between Native and non-Native cultures, with the game not always meaning the same things to the peoples who enjoy it. In the words of a Mohawk faith healer: "We played it with all our life force ... We ran from field to village, through streams and woods. There were few rules and no boundaries. Our bodies were unprotected and we invoked the spirits of the swift and powerful animals to guide us."

Sporting goods store founder Albert Spalding said categorically that lacrosse is "the very best game that was ever played."

In 1934, player and poet Fred Jacobs put it this way:

> Maybe you shed a tooth or two, your skin is not always
> whole
> But it's worth it when you grab the ball and bang in
> the winning goal.

11

Incident at Rankin Inlet

Stories tend not to unfold in the Arctic the same way they do in the South. The contours are different, the outcomes are different, too, and the results are usually incomprehensible. At one time off Rankin Inlet, an Inuit woman in a small boat needed to relieve herself. Her husband begged her not to urinate in the water, arguing that this would offend the gods. Desperate, she called upon a spirit to help her. The spirit agreed to help, but demanded the woman forfeit her life.

In the South, it would be no deal. But in the Arctic, for reasons that are hard to fathom, the woman agreed. The spirit at once transformed a nearby iceberg into an island for her convenience, and, having relieved herself, she died moments later while crawling on her hands and knees on the cobble beach.

Today this shining piece of rock is called Marble Island. Made almost entirely of quartz, it glows a brilliant white beneath clear skies. In 1721, for reasons that are not known, a gold-seeking expedition led by James Knight, consisting of two ships and twenty-five men, landed on this island. During the course of the next two years they disappeared off the face of the earth. It seems that scurvy, starvation, and mortal conflict with the "Eskemays," turned this site into one of the grimmest locations in the history of Northern exploration. Today on the western tip of the island, whales are still flensed by men and women wielding *sivaks* and *ulus*, the gendered knives of the Inuit. Visitors to this island approach on their hands and knees in deference to a legendary woman who needed to pee and perhaps to the many others who have died horrible deaths here, and whose stories have never been told.

On the mainland twenty miles west of this island is a settlement named Rankin Inlet. In a rock field just outside of town, carcasses of dogs are scattered about in various stages of decomposition. Some have the red, plastic casing of a shotgun shell lying next to them. Scampering everywhere are the *sik sik*, a nervous, corpulent ground squirrel the size of a terrier and the preferred target of Inuit boys who hurl stones at them with careless, but astonishing accuracy.

Out on the land sit several rusted compressors with evidence of people having lived in them; a few berths bolted to the walls, a dog carcass on the bottom, and three or four small windows blow-torched out of the side, cut small enough to keep the polar bears from getting in. One has an enormous television antenna fixed to it. Other examples of Inuit adaptability are near at hand, including the cracked Plexiglas windshield of a snowmobile sewn exquisitely back together with nylon gut. This sort of ingenuity is legendary in the Arctic. In the 1950s an Inuk was said to have opened the back of a .35-millimetre camera for a traveller, and fixed the broken timing mechanism, having up to that moment never seen a camera in his life.

It is a land that demands considerable ingenuity and does not tolerate mistakes. In 1847 when Franklin's men, already mad from lead poisoning, attempted to remove their own boots, they discovered their toes came off with them.

* * *

Rankin Inlet is named after British naval officer, John Rankin. History remembers him as the man who lied about the Northwest Passage, swearing not only that it existed at this latitude (64), but that Christopher Middleton, his commanding officer and one of history's finest navigators, was deliberately concealing it. Middleton was the first man to successfully navigate using a Hadley's quadrant and was, in the end, ruined by Rankin's deliberate and false accusations.

Today Rankin Inlet is a windswept settlement of prefabricated buildings clustered on the rocks. The wind is legendary and scours the ancient bedrock as it vents itself continuously southward. There are no flags in Rankin Inlet, only half flags, the ends torn to shreds. It is said here that flags snapping loudly but straight out indicate winds of thirty-five kilometres. A snapping flag inclined upward means winds of more than thirty-five kilometres — enough, at least for some, to keep the boat off the waters. The boats themelves are scattered in clusters, like the houses, down by the waters of Hudson Bay, as if waiting for the tide to float them.

Unlike the neighbouring coastal communities of Arviat and Whale Cove, which were established in the fifties to save the Inuit from starvation following a change in the caribou migrations, Rankin Inlet began as a mining town. According the 1998 *Nunavut Handbook*, the Inuit were "very hard workers and much appreciated by the mine owners." This is tourist guide code for a place that has no tourism. In plain English it means that the Inuit men received half the wage of the white miners and were required to eat in separate lunchrooms. The mine closed in 1962. The giant headframe that dominated Rankin Inlet burnt to the ground in the mid-eighties. Today there is a nasty ongoing lawsuit concerning who exactly owns the rights to the land and the nickel.

The Northern Store, formerly owned by the Hudson's Bay Company, is a massive prefabricated shed that sells everything from T-shirts, five-gallon tubs of lard, and white rolled slabs of whale fat labeled *muktuk*. In a small stall off to the side is a combination pizza parlour, fried-chicken restaurant, and video store. An enormous walrus head is mounted above the videos. The place is packed with Inuit children. A few fries are getting eaten and more kids file in and look about the room the way grown men enter a tavern.

It's worth mentioning that Inuit children are granted a type of freedom that is rare in the South. At Iqaluit, following a dinner of frozen peas, instant mashed potatoes, and fresh caribou, I watched a powerful boy of five begin to push an abandoned stereo console across the living room floor. The women played cards and smoked cigarettes. The men smoked and watched, transfixed, a documentary on the hunting techniques of large jungle cats. They had watched this same video many times. Finally the boy, with a great deal of proud grunting, managed to shoulder the cabinet to the lip of the landing and send it crashing down a flight a stairs. The noise was deafening. No one in the room even looked up. Another time, at Arviat, a seven-year-old boy, clutching a ticket, boarded a twin-prop Saab on which I was travelling and took a seat. The flight attendant spent ten minutes attempting, in English, to find out who he was. "Who's your mommy?" she asked repeatedly. But the boy did not speak English, he spoke Inuktitut. Following some tense discussion with the captain, the plane, against regulations, departed. After skidding sideways through ferocious Arctic "bubbles," as the first officer called them, with a grin, the plane landed forty minutes later at Rankin Inlet. The little Inuit boy had played unconcernedly throughout with a plastic spoon. At Rankin Inlet he skipped down the runway and ran home.

A number of these boys and girls are crowded into the only fast-food place in Rankin Inlet and making a great deal of noise. Mostly it's in Inuktitut, although a few phrases of English filter through: "Johnny, you rich man now, hey? You rich man?" I manage to buy a hamburger, but this accomplishment is marred by my insistence on mustard. The girl behind the counter views my request with some skepticism. She sees no reason for putting mustard on a hamburger; she sees little reason for a hamburger. There is a good chance she prefers *Igunaq*, walrus meat aged three months under a rock and eaten raw, preferably off a sheet of plywood on the gymnasium floor at the community centre. She has no fond memories associated with a hamburger. After engaging in a whispered conversation with her co-worker she eventually provides me, proudly, with — salt.

I am seated at a plastic table eating my salted hamburger when I notice the girl. She is two years old and big, with black, tangled hair and she's staring at me. Either she is staring at me because I am *qallnaat* — white people, or she's staring at me because I have red hair. It must be the hair. There have been *qallnaat* since 1540 when fool's gold brought Martin Frobisher and a crew of twelve boys, each armed with a jackknife, a *poignard*, and a Bible, to fight the heathens. It was the crucial and telling moment of contact. The English crew lifted a curious *Esquimeau* from his *kayak*. In the struggle, the terrified man bit his own tongue off. Later the Englishmen touched land at Baffin Island and used an inflated walrus bladder to play soccer against a group of Inuit. (The English won in a close match, but apparently they cheated.)

The girl is quite mesmerized. She is sucking on what appears to be a large Slurpee and in her left hand she clutches a penny. It's the penny that fascinates her now. She presses it between her fingers as though it were a totem possessing magical power. She senses the magic in it, pulsating in her hand. Suddenly, in the way of children, the focus changes. She is no longer interested in the penny; there are other people, dozens of them. She knows every one of them. There is no one living in Rankin Inlet she does not know — a few *qallnaat*, perhaps, like me. Otherwise the people come in, go out, laugh, step around her, over her. In the midst of this activity her grip on the penny loosens. It falls to the ground and rolls tantalizingly down the aisle.

I've seen this story before. I've seen it in film clips and in life, perhaps even in dreams. I know its shape and I know how it ends. I will get up and rescue the penny. In a gesture of benevolence I will then hand it back to her. Her mouth will detach from the Slurpee and she will smile gratefully at me. The large man, her father, will nod agreeably. By this act I will fit in. I will demonstrate the truth of Waugh's dictum that "the tourist is always the *other* fellow," never me. Somehow the gesture will be made more touching by the valuelessness of the coin up here, where a stale lettuce the size of a baseball costs four dollars. My role is clear.

Instead I remain firmly seated, eating a salted hamburger. The tyranny of the story is not absolute here. It holds no sway in the Arctic. Here a woman forfeits her life so as not to pee in the water. A man sits in the corner ten feet away, his face covered with stitches. Six weeks ago a polar bear removed the flesh from his skull. I'm told his face "was hanging off." Apparently this is what a polar bear does: attempts to crack a man's skull the way it cracks the head of a seal. The man's grandmother was killed in the attack. He escaped with a boy in a small boat. It was the third time in his life that he had been attacked by a polar bear. Now he's eating a slice of pizza next to a rack of videos. Above him hangs an enormous stuffed walrus head. This is not the South and stories do not have their same contours here. Anyone foolish enough to come here has a consular duty not to impose them.

I sit watching the penny roll in a very tantalizing way down the aisle where finally it stops. From the girl comes no disappointed wail. Her penny has escaped; it lies six feet away from her on the floor. She has a Slurpee, a roomful of people, the glinting shafts of language, laughter, the smell of lard bubbling in the vats. All of this presses in on her. She has lost interest in the penny and turns away. The urge to intercede and to do something has washed over me and passed. I've withstood it and done nothing. Because of that I'm free to watch the story unfold the way it's meant to.

It turns out that another man sitting at another plastic table has his own ambitions on the penny. He's making a move for it, but his moves are laboured. The man suffers from a serious skeletal injury; his legs and his spine are twisted. The complex gestures required for him to unfold his legs are excruciating to watch. The legs respond slowly. At one point he's forced to use his hands to move them. He lays one leg to the ground and cocks it awkwardly to accommodate the other. A grimace of pain flashes across his lips. He is virtually lying on the floor where the penny is. I'm holding my breath for the man.

The same painful gestures are executed in reverse to get himself back up. This is done gradually, in stages. He lifts up the penny from the ground and pantomimes a story that is far more profound than any I could have played a part in. He is a man sprawled in pain on the floor beneath a stuffed walrus head. Through a series of agonizing gestures he retrieves a penny that belongs to a very little girl.

The man rises to his feet, folds the penny in his hand and then, with a quick look around, shoves it into his pocket and limps from the building.

12

Canada 1912:
The Sinking of the Mayflower

In 1912 Stephen Leacock published his famous "sunshine sketches" of a small Canadian town, a satiric tribute to a way of life that was already dying. In the same year, in the vanishing pinewoods of the Ontario north, an Englishman named Archie Belaney was transforming desperately into "a half-breed Apache" known as Grey Owl, beginning a journey out of one civilization and into another. Across the country in Vancouver, cancer was claiming the life of E. Pauline Johnson, the Mohawk Princess and *de facto* mother of the frontier age. In Quebec a twenty-three-year-old Louis Hemon had finished his masterpiece *Maria Chapdelaine* and was embarking west on a journey that would leave him struck dead by a train in Chapleau, Ontario, before his book saw print. In English-speaking Canada, patriotic fervour favoured war against the Prussians, and, in the Local Option town of Yorkton, Saskatchewan, the body of young John Herman Brown was being shipped east by train to Barry's Bay, Ontario.

This unheralded event, taking place on a cold November morning, would culminate in the greatest inland marine disaster in Canadian history, and toll the final hours of pioneer Canada.

II

At the turn of the century, the shipping of bodies by train was a common occurrence and John Herman Brown was just one of many corpses crossing the country in this manner. A native of Renfrew County near Ottawa, he had moved out west a year earlier, living with his sister and the local man she had married — a man named Robert Pachal. On the morning of November 7, John Brown was discovered in the bushes of a prairie slough with a bullet hole in his head, his rifle lying in his lap. The *Yorkton Enterprise* called the death "mysterious" — likely a hunting accident — and grouped it with the numerous other deaths of the week. These included W.F. Good, who had "the wheels of a heavily loaded wagon pass over him, breaking his neck," and three Galicians "who fought each other with pitchforks" one of whom was "thrown into a separator while it was in operation."

The body of John Herman Brown was placed in a coffin and encased in a pine deal box. Under the guardianship of his sister's husband, it was transported three days by train back to Renfrew County for burial. Upon arriving at Barry's Bay, a busy timber town in northeastern Ontario, Robert Pachal made use of a local telephone to reach a relative of the deceased man, fifteen miles west at Combermere.

Although the telephone had been in use for some years, it was only recently that a skeptical public had become convinced that tuberculosis could not be spread through the wires. A great deal of concern had also made its way into print about the telephone being used by women. It was wondered, publicly, what women could have to say to each other that justified the use of a telephone.

The telephone system of Combermere, Ontario, was run by a man named Paddy O'Brien. Conceivably it was O'Brien who patched the call through to William Boehme, a neighbour and local tailor, related to the dead man, and to Robert Pachal by his marriage to Miss Brown. History has no record of what words those two men exchanged, although their communication proved fateful. Almost certainly they discussed the details of transporting John Herman Brown's body the remaining fifteen miles to Combermere. The road, nothing more than a cart trail and a morass of November mud, was out of the question: a coffin could not be transported by stage across that road. William Boehme suggested another method. He would get his friend John Hudson to sail the *Mayflower* up to Barry's Bay and they would bring back the coffin that way.

III

John Hudson was a classic figure of his era and wore the handlebar moustache to prove it. A timberman, an innkeeper, a ship owner, a reeve of Radcliffe Township, and a man who, reportedly, had not been sober in twelve months, he also held the somewhat rare distinction of being a Protestant man married to a Catholic woman.

Hudson, like many men in the timberfields of Ontario, also had a fondness for making money. Even though the *Mayflower* was docked for the winter, the owner quickly reassembled his crew. That crew consisted of Hudson's acting captain and pilot, Aaron Parcher, a youthful farmer from Combermere, and a teenaged orphan boy named Tommy Delaney, a fireman, whose job it was to keep the boiler stoked with pine slabs. Also on board to lend assistance with the coffin were William Boehme, the tailor; Paddy O'Brien; and William Murphy, a friend of O'Brien's.

At approximately 5:00 p.m. on the November 12, 1912, the familiar, square-nosed bow of the *Mayflower* left the dock at

Combermere. She was not an elegant boat, resembling, at best, a seventy-foot shoebox with a clapboard pilot house and a noisy paddlewheel at the stern. Built mainly to haul corundum from the now vanished mine at Craigmont across the long expanse of Lake Kamaniskeg, she also routinely transported passengers, although John Hudson had no licence to do so, and had recently sworn to a government inspector that he would stop. In 1910, in what might have been the most raucous drunk-ups in the history of Renfrew County — a county in which raucous drunk-ups were not unknown — she took out the entire Barry's Bay baseball club for an overnight party after winning the Ottawa Valley Championship. She'd run aground at least once and had nearly gone over in the wind with a high-ranking church official on board. She was sometimes cuttingly referred to as "the Jewel of Kamaniskeg."

Despite her appearance, to see the *Mayflower* straining beneath the hills of the Madawaska Valley, clouds scudding over top and black smoke from her stack scribbling the sky, would have been a comforting and unforgettable sight. Today the image conjures a relic of the vanishing world of the late frontier, when unregulated, unlicensed steamboats ran roughshod across the fresh inland lakes of Canada by the thousands. It was an era of flamboyant ill-trained captains and rogue steamers. It was an era that the *Mayflower* herself would help bring to an end.

IV

Two hours after leaving her home base at Combermere, the *Mayflower* nudged against the wharf at Barry's Bay. According to eyewitnesses it arrived with a bang — too much of a bang — fuelling more speculation that John Hudson was again less than sober.

As that was happening it is likely that Robert Pachal sat eating dinner in the Balmoral Hotel, a storied, almost legendary timberman's establishment, which still stands today. When it was finished, he boarded the steamboat, just arrived at the dock, a few hundred yards away. The box containing John Herman Brown's coffin was placed on deck at the bow, where the horse and buggy would usually go, and, presumably, an exhausted Pachal found a crate to sit on amid the jumble and the grime of the cargo hold.

Seated with this young stranger from the west was an eighty-year-old woman, Mrs. McWhirter. She was, according to newspapers, "a cripple." In 1912 that term encompassed a range of limb problems, including limping. A man with a missing limb was confidently termed by newspapermen a "peg leg." Eighty years old and "a cripple," Mrs. McWhirter was obviously not an invalid, having completed a train and buggy trip through the hills of the Madawaska Valley. Exactly where she was going, or even coming from, is not clear from the newspaper accounts. It was at Barry's Bay that well-meaning locals convinced her that the road to Combermere would leave her "badly shaken up … and would not be very pleasant for one of her mature age." It was strongly recommended she take Hudson's steamer, the *Mayflower*, instead. Reportedly she boarded in "the best of health and spirits."

Getting on with her were four commercial travellers from Ottawa. Young, brash, talkative, urbane, athletic, and well-dressed, newspaper photographs of the day show their faces cleanly shaved in the city manner for young men. They were Gordon Peverley, John Imlach, Joseph Harper, and Gordon Bothwell, "travellers" for such Ottawa companies as the Canadian Consolidated Rubber Co., the Cortecelli Silk Co., the F.J. Castle Co., and the General Supply Company. These were the youthful emissaries of the future, bringing modern, mass-produced city goods out to the hinterland. All of them had prior plans to take a stage or train to other villages. The unscheduled, out-of-season appearance of the *Mayflower* changed that and they boarded it gratefully, if not a little indignantly, after paying what was then considered an extortive fee of $1.50 for a one-way ride.

Of the remaining men, four were there to insure the casket containing John Herman Brown reached its final resting place in the hills of Schutt, Ontario. Robert Pachal, the Saskatchewan resident who accompanied the casket east, was twenty-five years old and born on Christmas Day. Of German-speaking Russian origins, his family had immigrated to Canada as part of Clifford Sifton's ambitious scheme to populate the prairies. It was a scheme that included immigration agents paid by the head, colourful posters printed by the millions, dubious claims, and outright lies. The more astonishing of these was the insistence that the mean temperature of prairie winters was higher than Florida. Lacking confidence in his own propaganda, Sifton eventually instituted a ban on publishing — in Europe — the winter temperatures of the Canadian prairies.

According to the *Yorkton Enterprise*, Pachal was a well-known citizen of Yorkton with a large circle of friends, who had been brought to the area "while an infant in arms." He had left behind him Miss Brown, his wife of three years, and a two-year-old infant daughter. Presumably, with the Browns' deceased son in his care, he would be meeting his wife's family for the first time.

Down there in the cargo hold, sharing that brief, tragic journey, was Paddy O'Brien, operator of the Combermere telephone exchange. Having failed to master writing or reading, he had cleverly moved into the telephonic industry, perhaps in the belief that such skills would not be required there. An avuncular white-haired man with thick glasses, he too was a reeve of Radcliffe township, the proprietor of his own hotel, and had signed the deed to his concession property with an *X*. For him the trip was either a favour to John Hudson, or the Brown family, or both. Along with him was a friend, William Murphy, whose sister, aged seventeen, had died of diphtheria and is today buried next to him in a plot of the Rockingham Church, a tiny, pine board structure erected in 1846 and still standing. Her tombstone carries the somewhat gloomy inscription: *Be ye also ready*.

Little known also is William Boehme, an elegant wide-eared man with tuft-like eyebrows and swept-back hair. A local tailor, he too was a member, along with John Hudson and Paddy O'Brien, of the Radcliffe council. It seemingly was Boehme's decision, after talking on the telephone to Robert Pachal, to request that the *Mayflower* be activated for a last trip up "the Bay," and back.

Acting captain and pilot of the *Mayflower* was Aaron Parcher. A fair-haired young man with a guileless face, he was a farmer by trade and almost certainly lacked any marine training. Married with two children he, tragically, had purchased farmland near Kirkland Lake and was only days away from moving his family up there.

V

At approximately 7:00 p.m., on Tuesday, November 12, under a mounting wind, the *Mayflower* left the federal wharf at Barry's Bay and began steaming west toward Combermere. It held twelve people and a dead man in a casket — what a Toronto newspaper would later call "its cargo of human freight." Among those twelve people resided the triumphs, hopes, knowledge, failures, and history of a young nation. On board were those who had fished lake trout using a bit of red cloth as bait. Others had greased the axle of an automobile with bear fat. Some had entered the mysterious confines of a moving picture show, or scraped a chair in the smoke-filled basement of a Sons of Temperance meeting. One belonged to a Masonic lodge. Another favoured the vote for women. Possibly one of them had witnessed "a brazen lady" light up a cigarette in the Palm Room of the Château Laurier, a scandal which, that same week, made the front page of the Ottawa papers.

They were husbands and hunters, speechifiers, moonshiners, grandmothers, bachelors, tailors, orphans, and alcoholics. They belonged to that group of settlers who had taken down the largest pine forest on the face of the earth. They were a people who had killed bears and been killed by bears. They were tough, unsentimental country folk who drank a mixture of turpentine mixed with brown sugar to cure a sore throat. They boiled raspberry leaves to cure the ailments of women. They witnessed forest fires in which the sun was blotted out for a week.

Crowded around the boiler in the hold of that old boat, they mingled together in a type of comradeship that can only be guessed at. Perhaps they looked on with haughty distrust at the city fellows, those four commercial travellers, wearing "store boughts" and no hair on their faces. Perhaps a flask of whiskey made its way discreetly from man to man, for medicinal purposes only. Perhaps they swapped tales and sang a popular, telling verse from "Green Martin": "The world is round and runs on wheels/Death is thing that everyone feels."

What is known for sure is that approximately five minutes before nine o'clock, with the wind rising considerably, and the snow coming down, Gordon Peverley, a traveller for the Corticelli Silk Co., caught the attention of the young boy stoking the boiler and shouted:

"What time will we get to Combermere?"

"What time would it be now, then?" asked the boy.

"Getting on to nine o'clock."

"Get there about ten o'clock," answered the boy.

Five minutes later the ice cold water of Kamaniskeg came rushing in from both sides at the stern, and the *Mayflower* went down.

VI

In the ensuing hours, less than a hundred yards from shore, nine people lost their lives. Owner John Hudson drowned attempting to release the pressure off the boiler to stop it from exploding. Mrs. McWhirter, eighty years old and infirm, did not make it out of the cabin. According to Gordon Peverley, "The water came in with such a rush that we couldn't get near her." A kerosene lamp crashed to the water and was doused, leaving only blackness; what an Ottawa newspaper called "the terror of a Stygian darkness."

Only one thing managed to float safely from the sinking vessel — the rough pine box encasing the casket of John Herman Brown. Immediately the three commercial travellers, Imlach, Harper, and Peverley, draped themselves, groaning, across this desperate life raft. The tailor William Boehme, surfaced nearby, but could not make his way toward them and drowned. Paddy O'Brien, despite his age and the freezing water, somehow thrashed his way to the coffin box, leaving four men clinging to it. A small section of *the Mayflower*, the roof of the pilothouse, protruded from the water. Eerily, a lamp still glowed inside. Clung piteously to the flagpole was the boy fireman, Thomas Delaney, and beneath him, Mr. William Murphy of Rockingham. "[The boy] said he was too cold and he couldn't swim, and he was afraid to jump and he drifted away from us," described Peverley. William Murphy, too exhausted to hang on, "gave up hope and sank."

Acting Captain Aaron Parcher fixed a lifebelt around himself and hollered out that he would swim to shore, to his father's farm on a spit of land, and bring out help. He never made it. The lone, terrified voice of Robert Pachal, the stranger from the west, could be heard screaming through the blackness. Scotty Bothwell, the fourth commercial traveller, ironically, a prize-winning swimmer, perished in an unseen manner. His body was not found for months afterwards.

It was now approximately 9:15 in the evening. Four men were adrift on a coffin box. A gale force wind slashed their faces. Snow beat down on them. A slush of ice was beginning to form on the surface of the lake, making a sickening and terrifying rustling noise. Paddy O'Brien "had lost his head" and periodically broke out into incoherent screaming.

For three impossible and appalling hours they drifted. Finally, Gordon Peverley, in fit of desperation, kicked off his boots, untied his necktie, which he wrapped around his own wrist and the wrist of Joseph Harper, who could no longer hang on, and began swimming blindly toward what looked like the silhouette of a tree, followed by Imlach and O'Brien. "Ten minutes later I touched bottom and clambered ashore." They had landed on what was then called Gull Island, a tiny outcrop of rock and stunted cedars. A few minutes later, an exhausted and broken Paddy O'Brien died in Peverley's arms. "The gurgle came out of his throat and then he was gone," Peverley later told an inquest. He quickly removed O'Brien's boots and put them on his own feet.

Nothing would come easy for these three youthful city men. Knowing they would die without a fire, they attempted to light one using an automatic cigarette lighter. The wick was soaked through and would not ignite, so they began to blow on it in an effort to dry it out. They blew for two hours. Eventually a fire was started and they survived the first night by slapping each other's faces to prevent themselves from falling asleep and passing about the one winter coat amongst themselves. The following morning a steamboat, the *Ruby,* sailed past, but did not see their frantic waving. It returned in the afternoon and again did not see them.

Toward dusk that evening, a young boy, walking on shore, saw a body floating in the water. He rushed home to tell his father, who paddled out with a canoe to investigate. The man, a farmer named Silas Parcher, reached the corpse and turned it over, only to find himself staring into the face of his own son. Far off on a small island, he discerned a man waving a branch and realized what had happened. The older Parcher canoed home and hurried off to the village of Combermere for help. That evening a rescue party was sent to the island. The three surviving men, after spending three hours in the water, and almost twenty more on snow-clogged rock island, were rescued and taken to a Combermere hotel which until the previous night had been owned by John Hudson. There one of them told a reporter, "We could not have been treated whiter."

"Here were are enjoying a smoke apparently little the worse for our experience," expanded the phlegmatic Gordon Peverley.

Not one country person survived the tragedy. Their monuments, today, are found in cemeteries dotting the Madawaska Valley. Robert Pachal, who died transporting a coffin east, would not be sent home. He is buried next to John Herman Brown in the alpine hills of Schutt, Ontario. William Murphy lies next to his sister in the hills of Rockingham. Aaron Parcher, John Hudson, and Paddy O'Brien lie close together in Combermere cemeteries. All of their tombstones bear that ominous date, November 12, 1912, when nine country people and the way of life they had known vanished forever beneath the surface of a freshwater lake.

VII

In February 1913, a federal inquiry headed by Justice Pringle finished its work. Evidence heard at the inquiry included an unsigned and contemptuous letter stating that John Hudson, the owner, "has not been known to have been sober for twelve months." The actual reasons for the sinking were more prosaic. Hudson had lately shortened the buckets on the paddlewheel to prevent the *Mayflower* from running aground in the shallows. This shortening produced more strain on the hull, particularly in high wind. That strain, on November 12, caused the hull planks at the stern to open a finger-width, permitting the water to flood in. The weight of the iron boiler, situated at the stern, forced the boat to dip suddenly, causing the water to rush in farther until, in a matter of minutes, she sank.

Based on Pringle's report, the federal government would soon make changes to the inland shipping laws, noticeably those laws governing the requirements for lifeboats, and the manner and frequency with which inland marine vessels would be inspected and overhauled. The report concluded with an opinion likely shared by most county residents; "As I heard many rumours regarding John Hudson, I think it only fair to say ... that on the night in question, he was perfectly competent to take charge of the *Mayflower*, and that both Delaney and Parcher were competent men."

The sinking of the *Mayflower* made front-page news across North America. The macabre "Saved by a Casket" angle proved irresistible to newspapermen and a populace already primed by the tragedy of the *Titanic*. Sixty years later it would attract the attention of "Ripley's Believe It Or Not," and resurface, for one morning, the subject of a syndicated cartoon — "The Corpse That Saved Three Men from Drowning!"

The *Mayflower* sinking remains the largest single loss of life in Renfrew County and the largest inland marine disaster in Canadian history. Gull Island, where three urbane and youthful commercial travellers made a desperate stand, slapping each other's faces in order to stay awake, has been renamed Mayflower Island. It is briefly visible from the car on Highway 62, rising from the sapphire-coloured surface of Lake Kamaniskeg. Today, in the summer, surfboarders, Sea Doo-ers and water-skiers race obliviously overhead, while the *Mayflower*, long settled in the silt, lies just out of sight in twenty-five feet of water.

13

"Et By a Wolf":
The Origins and Shape of Northern Humour (Part 1)

One of the earliest known witticisms recorded in English Canada took place in 1817 in the town of Hamilton. It occurred in a prison and was uttered by a debtor confined there. The man, shackled at both feet and chained to an iron ring in the floor, offered a protest against the cold. Pointing at the stove, he warned his jailor, "either you get that fire up, or I'm leavin."

In 1817 this comment was thought funny enough to be preserved in memory, then finally copied on paper. Like almost all northern humour, it is based on hardship, and like almost all northern humour it insists that only through a blind and proud stupidity can those hardships be survived or at least endured.

A half century later near Denbigh, Ontario, timbermen sang a shanty song that celebrated the memory of a dead cook;

> When Sandy was livin' before he was dead
> He gave us good grillades to eat with our bread

Life, the lyric writer is good enough to inform us, is that brief, inconsequential thing that happens before we die.

This brutality in either grammar or logic, and often both, is the trademark of northern humour. It is heard again in a remark uttered by the editor of the *Sault Daily Star*. In 1925, James Curran attempted to prove once and for all that a wolf in the wild would not attack a human being, and offered one hundred dollars to any person who could prove conclusively he'd been set upon by a wolf. "Any man who says that he's been et by a wolf is a liar" wrote Curran. Another editor would remark that "the word 'et' is used under mild protest" although he admitted "it has greater stamina than the longer word." The remark, in fact, is one that Curran attributed to his alter ego, the fantastically wise, frequently quoted perennially pipe-smoking, "Old Sam Martin of Michipicoten."

This famous challenge was heard around the world and many rose to meet it. One of those who responded was a CPR foreman who claimed he was operating a jigger when a wolf leapt down from a rock, landed on the speeding machine, and attempted to eat him. It would seem the railwayman wrestled the wolf to the ground and leapt aboard an oncoming train. The story was judged "inconclusive" and the reward went unclaimed. In fact, no amount of evidence would seemingly convince editor Curran to give up his one hundred dollars. "Being in the news-paper business," suggested another editor, "he might possibly find rather urgent use for it." Dubious reports streamed in, or at least Curran claimed they did, from Paris, from Belfast, and even Hungary, where a pack of wolves had entered a church and "killed the entire congregation" or Rumania where wolves entered a villages "and left not a human being alive."

It was Curran's stated belief that, "If a hardy Algoma wolf won't eat anybody, the softer species father south probably won't either." He considered the Algoma wolf to be "almost as dangerous as the Algoma rabbit," and would later write a book titled *Wolves Don't Bite* in which he insisted there are things in Ontario that are more dangerous than the wolf, "for instance, the step ladder." In the end he concedes only one known victim of a wolf attack: "Little Red Riding Hood's grandmother."

From from wolf attacks to brute labour, from cholera to forest fires, from blackflies to hatchet wounds, northern humour is birthed out of everyday misery. Stripped of learning and sophistication, it is often oral humour, created not so much by the author, but by the innkeeper and the jailed debtor. Examples were to be found painted on boards, such as this one hanging from an old Ontario tavern in the early 1800s: GOOD FOOD AND ACCOMMODATION FOR BOTH MAN AND HORSE. Here the formal literacy of England has now given up hope and is already rotting in the bush.

Three quarters of a century later, Old World cleverness had all but given up the ghost. In 1913, a sign hung in the lobby of the Stag Hotel in Golden City, Ontario, stated succinctly: WE KNOW THIS HOTEL IS ON THE BUM. WHAT ABOUT YOURSELF? Today, in a small public park in Massey, Ontario, on a spit of land where the Aux Sable River meets the Mississagi, there is an old but functioning outhouse. On the side of it, painted in white, and spelled not altogether correctly, is the simple graffiti: NO ASSHOLES ALOWED.

This aggressive dimwittedness is what distinguishes Canadian humour from its English parent. The epigram, the witty remark as uttered by the cultured Englishman reveals just the opposite — the cleverness of the speaker. Two centuries ago Chief Justice Elmsley of old Toronto wrote to a friend: "There is no news here except the death of my Parrot who departed this life the day before yesterday without a will." This charming remark, though composed on North American soil, is still patently European humour, whimsical, privileged, and the product of a gentleman with too much time on his hand.

Similarly when Oscar Wilde stood among honeymooners atop Niagara Falls and proclaimed the great cataract to be "the bride's second biggest disappointment," he was revealing himself to be a man of extreme sophistication. Not only was he slandering the performance of Englishmen in the bedroom and scandalously implying Englishwomen might *care* about this sort of thing, he was also celebrating an urbane indifference to nature. The genius does not care about water crashing over rocks. In continental humour, the mind, the wit, and the execution of one's own superior intelligence is what matters. Nature has no place here. "Nature," as New York humorist Fran Lebowitz explains, is what happens between the hotel and the taxi.

In the North, however, nature *is* what matters. Nature causes the taxi to skid out of control, and burns the hotel to the ground. Rather than being tedious, nature is fast and brutal and makes a mockery of sophistication; even of common sense. In the deadly cold and yawning loneliness of the North, suicide beckons, but offers no real solution. As Stephen Leacock helpfully informs us, we should probably not commit suicide because "It often involves serious consequences …"

A good argument can be made that the shape and originality of Northern wit is the result of a hard-boiled immigrant experience grafted onto the indigenous humour of the First Peoples. "The Indian," wrote Peter Spohn in 1811, "has a great sense of humour, loving jests, games, dancing, and merry-making." Unfortunately, we do not possess an extensive record of what these jests were. Possibly it was a humour expressed in physical language, or song.

Just as possibly it was a dry, stoical, resignation to the hardships of northern life, expressed with delicious crudity.

In 1850, George Copway, whose own writings are crushingly tedious, recorded the following "joke," which took place between two Ojibway chiefs at a Washington dinner. Unaccustomed to the white man's table, one chief swallowed a bowl of mustard. Seeing the tears stream from his eyes, his companion asked "Brother why do you weep?"

The chief answered, "I am thinking about my son who was killed in battle." The second chief swallowed his own bowl of mustard and also began to cry. The first asked, "And why do you weep?"

"Because," the chief answered, "*you* were not killed in battle along with your son!"

More recently the story is told of an Inuit elder being pestered by a visiting city journalist. The man, on assignment in Baffin Island, had grown deathly afraid of polar bears and demanded to know what he was supposed to do if attacked by one. The old Inuk gave the matter some thought, folded his arms, and answered sagely, "Use your common sense." The response reveals the chasm between two cultures, one in which "using your common sense," is a euphemism for dying an extremely gruesome death.

The humour of the North is also the humour of alcohol. There is hardly any northern or frontier humour that is not heavily soused in it.

Remove the drinking jokes from Leacock's *Sunshine Sketches of a Little Town* and not fifty pages would be left. The same observation can be made of the American humourist, O. Henry, who opened one of his drinking stories with the memorable line, "Baldy Woods reached for the bottle, and got it."

The line fits neatly alongside Leacock's boozy observation, "You know, I think, the peculiar walk of a man with two bottles of whiskey in the inside pockets of a linen coat." Here is heard the grammatical contortions that sound the pulse of northern humour. It is heard again when he concludes that a certain picnic cooler must be full of sandwiches because — "I think I can hear them clinking."

Often northern humour appears in unlikely places. The *Calgary Eye Opener* once suggested that "a man driven to drink, usually has to walk home." When the famous distiller Hiram Walker passed away, a newsman who wrote Walker's obituary had to the gall to conclude: "We are pleased to note that his spirit is still with us."

These sorts of liberties are a defining trademark of northern wit, regardless of whether they take place on the U.S. or Canadian side of the border. In 1980, the town council of Eagle Harbour, Michigan, on the south side of Lake Superior, found it necessary to spend thirty thousand dollars to replace the local fog horn. A grumpy councillor complained, "Thirty thousand dollars for a new fog horn, and *we've still got fog.*"

The American wit Josh Billings invoked a similar grammatical audacity when he lamented the poverty of artists, Pauline Johnson in particular. When it came to art, Billings noted, the public had a tendency to provide "too much epitaphy, and not enough taffy."

Eventually this sort of grammatical freedom would be eclipsed by a new generation of men and women; writers, editors, critics who fawned on Europe, longed for New York, and aped the styles of London in a desperate attempt to appear sophisticated. The pages of Canadian magazines would soon fill with their civilized yappings and the age of indoor writing would begin.

The Golden Age of the North and of northern funny men was coming to an end. No longer would people compose and exchange such flawless couplets as:

My name is Johnny Hall
And I'm from Montreal

They would not depart from each other with the benediction, "May your roof not cave in." Nor would they tell the tale of Paddy Garvey who went "up the Karcajoo" carrying an iron stove and leading a pregnant sow on a rope. Unfortunately the sow gave birth, forcing Paddy to chase the newborn piglets around the forest while lugging a cast iron stove on his afflicted back. Today the new and sophisticated Canadian would simply *put the stove down.*

But before that happened, this drunken wit of the Ottawa Valley was to get off one last ringing toast to northern humour. Staggering home one night in a drunken stupor, Paddy Garvey was confronted by the village priest. "Drunk again, Paddy?" the priest demanded. To which the blithe Irishman answered, "Me too father, me too."

14

"Et By a Wolf":
The Origins and Shape of Northern Humour (Part 2)

Following the publication of an earlier version of this piece in what was then called *The Beaver: Canada's History Magazine*, I received a lengthy, handwritten letter from a Lombard Avenue address in Winnipeg. It is reprinted here in full as a chastisement to Mr. James Curran and myself, and seems to prove that editor Curran's dismissal of the wolf story was premature and that Mr. Curran was more intent on keeping his hundred dollars than in giving it away:

> Dear Sir:
> I was interested in reading your article on p. 21 of your Oct-Nov issue of the Beaver re origins of Northern Humour, especially the paragraph about the wolf attacking the sectionman, as I was the front end trainman of the train involved.
>
> I found this article humorously far-fetched from reality. Being on the engine when the engineer applied the brakes I asked why he was stopping and he said, "there's a sectionman fighting with a wolf." So I backed

up to the spot and the fireman and I jumped off with pick and shaker bar. I hit the wolf on the head with the the pick & fireman Grier hit it with the shaker bar. This finished the wolf.

My understanding of the episode was that Mike Duziak was patrolling his velosopede [*sic*] when he took it off the rail to let our train go by. While waiting on the right-of-way-between track and bush the emaciated wolf jumped him. Mike had lost his hatchet & only had a dead branch in his hand fending off the wolf. Both were winded. We put the wolf on the cowcatcher and took it to Chapleau where we notified V. Crichton of the Lands & Forest who immediately walked to Poulin to verify the story by observing the foot & animal tracks before it snowed again. He wrote an account of it to the Biology Dept. of the Lands & Forests & it was printed in the Journal of Mamology with the Public Archives Library in Ottawa. In one of my visits to Ottawa I looked it up in the Public Library & it was there!

Another engineer Joe Delaney, challenged Mr. Curran of the Sault Star with this episode but Mr. Curran rescinded his offer. My mate on that trip was Willie Fartin, still living in the same retirement home as I, and vividly remembers the episode.

John Way-White
Member 1ZBZ97

A blow-by-blow description of this encounter between train crew and wolf appeared in the *Journal of Mamology*, Volume 28, No. 3 August 1947, pages 294–95.

15

Freak Show

On the evening of September 15, 1885, a Northern Trunk freight train driven at high speeds by engineer William Burnip, crossed Arthur Street in downtown St. Thomas, Ontario, and struck and killed a large elephant. This was not the sort of elephant usually found in St. Thomas, not even on nights when the circus passed through. This was the most celebrated animal on the face of the earth, the one creature, with the exception of Mickey Mouse, to eventually have its name canonized in dictionaries of the English language. This particular pachyderm was Jumbo, backbone of P.T. Barnum's "Greatest Show on Earth," and star of the most remarkable freak show to pitch a tent on Canadian soil.

Prior to its arrival in North America Jumbo, "The Children's Pet," had lived eighteen years in London, England, where 1,250,000 children, including a youthful Winston Churchill, had ridden on his back. So had Theodore Roosevelt. When British reporters learned that Jumbo was to become what they called the "chattel of a wandering showman," and an American at that, they were outraged. John Ruskin weighed in, and the London

Daily Telegraph was particularly indignant that Jumbo, instead of enjoying "friendly trots with British boys and girls," would now be forced "to amuse a Yankee mob" and eat peanuts and waffles.

II

Even without Jumbo, the history of elephants in the New World is a grim one. The first elephant to reach North American shores did so in 1796 aboard the privateer *America* and was killed for unknown reasons in 1822. In 1808, an African elephant was purchased in the nick of time from a New York slaughterhouse by businessman Hachaliah Bailey. "Old Bet," known today as the mother of America's carnival business, was put to work in a "circus" consisting of a dog, two pigs, and a horse. In July 1816, near Alfred, Maine, a religious fanatic shot the animal dead in the belief that it was morally wrong for poor farmers to spend hard-earned cash on the opportunity to see an elephant. In 1874, a 6,500-pound elephant, Norma Jean, was struck by lightning while parading through the town square of Oquawka, Illinois, and buried on the spot. In Indiana in 1901, Big Charley was shot dead after trampling its trainer to death. It too was buried on the spot. Elephants, not surprisingly, tend to be buried on the spot.

In 1903, American inventor and lunatic Thomas Edison arranged to have a zoo elephant named Topsy publicly electrocuted in Luna Park. Up to that point, Edison, in his bitter campaign to discredit the electrical theories of George Westinghouse, had been content to publicly electrocute cats and dogs. When Topsy, an enraged circus elephant, trampled its third trainer in three years, Edison offered to "execute" the animal in a way that would demonstrate once and for all his beliefs in the dangers of alternating current. The electrocution of Topsy was filmed by Edison's company, Biograph Studios, and apparently the footage can still be viewed at the Coney Island Museum.

III

Prior to that fateful September night when Jumbo was killed, St. Thomas, Ontario, was known, if at all, from a brief mention in Anna Brownell Jameson's *Winter Studies and Summer Rambles in Canada*, in which she ascribes to the town "three churches, one of which is very neat, and three taverns." It was also, by the time of Jumbo's death, the site of one of Canada's largest lunatic asylums. On the morning after, two hundred men armed with rope and tackle managed to topple the immense carcass down the embankment and clear the busy tracks. The Barnum and Bailey Circus, along with the human cannonball, the bearded lady, the tattooed man, the Hindoo snake charmer, the Feegee Mermaid (a monkey torso stitched to a fish tail), the New Zealand cannibal, and Joice Heth, the reputed 161-year-old nurse of George Washington, had already packed up and was steaming out of town without even a backward glance at its star attraction. That, as they say, is show biz.

With an eight-ton elephant lying dead on a railway embankment, residents of St. Thomas lost no time to emulating the hucksterism of Jumbo's famous owner. Five cents admission was charged to see Jumbo's carcass. Slivers were chipped off the tusks and sold. For two days Jumbo lay on the ground, at which point Barnum's personal taxidermists arrived from the United States to claim the skin and skeleton. Six local butchers were hired to cut up the meat. The viscera was burnt, and as the smell of broiled elephant wafted through St. Thomas, the *Daily Times* began selling its hastily printed Jumbo Memorial Tablets:

JUMBO
King of Elephants,
Died at ST. THOMAS, Sept. 15, 1885,
AGED 24 YEARS
The pillar of a people's hope,
The centre of the world's desire.

All that now remained was a flood of elephant grease, bottled and sold as a curative ointment for aches and pains. It is said that Cornell University paid forty dollars for Jumbo's heart.

Today Jumbo is no longer "the pillar of people's hope," nor perhaps is St. Thomas "the centre of the world's desire." Nonetheless, the Jumbo industry is still alive. Books have been written (at least two), websites maintained, and a fingernail-sized crystal Jumbo (currently out of stock) is available for $33 (U.S.).

In 1985, St. Thomas council commissioned a massive elephant sculpture to grace the downtown core. Sculpted in New Brunswick, the concrete Jumbo weighed thirty-eight tons and was transported 1,070 miles across the country. In an incident that seems to mirror the sorry history of elephants in North America, the legs were cut off so that it could clear the bridges dotting the Trans-Canada Highway. No tourist brochure mentions St. Thomas without immediately bringing up Jumbo — "the best known non-human that ever lived," as one local booster proudly put it.

IV

To some extent the abominable history of elephants in the new world is avenged by a strange curse that hovers over the Jumbo story. The man who captured Jumbo, a German carpenter, Johan Schmidt, died delirious in the Abyssinian highlands. Carl Akeley, sent by Barnum to retrieve Jumbo's skin, was himself later seriously trampled by an elephant and met his death in the Belgium Congo while tracking a bush antelope. His taxidermist colleague, Professor Henry Ward, was struck dead by a car in Chicago in 1906, becoming one of the New World's first recorded car-accident victims. Matthew Scott, Jumbo's personal handler, perished in a poorhouse in Bridgeport, Connecticut, in 1914. William Burnip, the engineer who drove the train on that fateful day, and later fashioned a tin elephant that he placed over the headlight of his deadly locomotive, was killed in the San Francisco earthquake of 1906.

As to Jumbo, or at least what was left him, finally, after four years of touring, the hide, which weighed 1,600 pounds, was placed in Barnum's Museum at Tufts College, Massachusetts. In 1975, the museum and all its contents was destroyed by fire caused by faulty wiring. It is said that a brave administrator waded into the smouldering ruins and collected some of Jumbo's ashes in, well, yes, an empty peanut butter jar. In fact, a hybrid jar; a fourteen-ounce Skippy jar, topped with a Crunchy Peter Pan lid.

Since 1975, Tufts College athletes have rubbed this jar for good luck prior to a big game.

16

Jack Miner:
The Man Who Would Have Dominion

In the first half of the twentieth century, he was ranked alongside William Shakespeare as one of the fifteen "greatest personages the world has ever known." *Maclean's* magazine placed him, more conservatively, as the fifth best-known man on the continent. The mayor of Detroit called him the "world's greatest naturalist." A Toronto professor compared him to Aristotle and found Aristotle wanting. In 1926, *Collier's* noted a distinct similarity to Francis of Assisi. His publishers insist he was the driving force behind the United Nations. To the rest of the English speaking world he was simply "Wild Goose Jack, the father of conservation."

In his newspaper columns, films, lectures, radio broadcasts, and books, he made himself known to millions. His story became mythical — an unschooled, illiterate, barefoot American boy learns his wisdom in the Canadian forest, feeds his family on the strength of his hunting, gives up hunting to rescue the Canadian goose from extinction, becomes the first conservationist, the first man to band birds, the first to establish a bird sanctuary — a man who changed not only the world's attitude toward nature, but nature itself. It is a story that two generations of schoolchildren were raised on, told so many times that for half a century it carried the unassailable truth of a folk tale.

His name was Jack Miner, born the fifth of ten children in 1865 at the hamlet of Dover Center, Ohio. At the age of thirteen, his family uprooted itself and relocated in Essex County, Ontario, on the north shore of Lake Erie, northeast of Detroit. A failed brick-making business is often given as the reason for the move, although the Miner family may have been attempting to put distance between Jack's father and his access to American liquor. Jack Miner would later suggest it was cheap land in the Kingsville area that precipitated the move; land owned by former American slaves who had travelled north on the perilous Underground Railway — "our darkies," Jack called them.

His youth, to the extent that it can be pieced together from his peculiar books, was spent schooling himself in the ways of the animals and the woods of southern Ontario. "I have never seen a human being possess better eyesight and hearing than I did, or one who could slip through the woods more noiselessly than I could," he boasted. According to Jack, he and his brother Ted were soon the delight of Essex County. Men came from miles to hear them sing. Men came from miles to watch them hunt. Jack is fond of letting his readers know that he was not a handsome boy, though somehow, like the Jack Miner story itself, his very ungainliness achieved heroic dimensions, capable of stopping "a through express train." Nor would he ever pass an opportunity to lovingly describe himself. "Reader, picture it if you can, the proud bashful smile on my freckled face."

This bashful, freckle-faced boy was also a ruthless market hunter. The term dates back four hundred years and designates a man who engages in the unlimited slaughter of animals for money. Jack Miner became expert at it. "Market hunting," he wrote, "is not a sport, it is murder in the first degree." According to Jack, he "soon out grew this murderous practice, and hunted for pleasure only."

At seventeen, Jack Miner was invited to guide a group of prominent Essex County gentlemen on a hunting trip. This story became central to the myth that sprang up around him: an uncouth, barefoot boy whose brilliance in the bush is recognized at once by his wealthy, influential betters — in his words, great men who "told clean stories," one of whom demands admiringly, "Young man, who taught you to disembowel a deer?" Within the hagiography of Wild Goose Jack it signifies young Jack's acceptance by his moral and social superiors. In the myths of the era, this little anecdote typifies the belief that a simple man leading a clean Christian life will be financially rewarded. It also predicts Jack Miner's life-long penchant for ingratiating himself with wealthy and prominent men. Seventeen was also the year that God "laid his hands on me and melted my revengeful heart into love." This conversion that Jack Miner is writing about is not a decision to stop hunting, but to stop hunting *on Sunday*, which by Canadian law was already illegal.

In 1888, he married a local woman, Loanna Wigle, whom he described as "one of the best Christian girls this world has ever known." That same year, the Ontario government banned the moose hunt, causing Jack to take his first moose-hunting trip in Quebec, which still permitted a season on the vanishing animal. Of this trip he wrote the partridges were "so tame we killed all we wanted with stones." The moose he and his party merely wounded were left to thrash around in the Quebec bush until they died.

In 1891, his first child, a son, was born, followed by a daughter, Pearl, in 1894. Three years later, as Jack Miner was planning another moose-hunting trip, young Pearl lost consciousness and died the same day. Of this tragedy he wrote: "All thoughts of going hunting or anywhere else except to her lonely little grave, had completely vanished from my mind." Two weeks later he was back in the Quebec bush, hunting moose.

A year later in a tragic hunting blunder, his brother Ted was shot in the back of the head at close range by a family friend and killed. Jack Miner, who carefully fostered an image of himself as the greatest hunter in Canada, was flushing the moose toward his brother when the accident occurred. How he could be involved in such a deadly mishap will never be known, but like most things in the Jack Miner story, the myth and man refuse to occupy the same space. "Don't ever ask me to go hunting," he stated after his brother's death. "I can never go hunting again." Jack got over his grief and several months later was back in the Quebec bush, hunting moose.

In 1900, Jack Miner, thirty-five years old, and, according to him, completely illiterate, began to conduct a Sunday school class. Jack's famed illiteracy is a cornerstone of the Miner myth, exemplifying both a belief in the conquering power of the individual will, and a deep-rooted suspicion of formal education. When asked by a young student if the moose lost its antlers, Jack Miner was in his element and wrote: "Stop right there, dear people, and think. Was there a man on the North American continent better qualified to answer this ... boy's question?" According to Jack he learned to read by listening to his students' recitations from the Bible. He was struck in particular by a quote from Genesis: "God gave man dominion over the fish of the sea, the fowls of the air and every living thing that creepeth upon it."

Jack had been teaching Sunday school for three years when his thirteen-year-old son Carl died of appendicitis. Jack's portrayal of this tragedy reads, unfortunately, as an epistle to his own greatness as a father. According to Jack his dying child was so overwhelmed by gratitude *to him* that his final words were: "Oh papa, how I wish I could have lived so I could have paid you back for some of your kindness."

About this time he began his first attempts to lure geese onto his property. In a frequently quoted passage, he describes a span of wild geese that flew overhead and recognized him, at once, as the enemy. Jack was so galled by this that he determined to do something about it. It is equally possible that behind the braggart was a broken, grief-stricken man who had grown up under the shadow of an alcoholic father, witnessed the death of two children and a beloved brother, and now felt the need to engage in the basic human impulse to feel something alive and warm come close to him.

In April 1905, after five years of fruitless efforts, eleven Canada geese finally landed on Jack Miner's property. With Jack's permission, five of them were promptly shot by neighbours. The following year, thirty-two geese arrived on the property. A third of them were shot. Jack also began raising ducks, clipping their wings, and selling their ducklings as live decoys to local hunters. It was under these circumstances that the Jack Miner Migratory Bird Sanctuary was born.

Shortly after this, something astonishing happened to Jack Miner — he became famous. Today it is difficult to understand exactly why, but in the early years of the twentieth century, the killing of wild animals still carried with it a potent moral symbolism — the Christian duty to cleanse a savage land. The wilderness writings of Grey Owl were a decade off and even the statutes of the newly formed Algonquin Park called virtuously for the annihilation of the wolf, the wildcat, "and other noxious animals." A person deliberately giving sanctuary to a wild goose or a duck had a "man-bites-dog" weirdness to it that the press found irresistible.

In 1909, Jack began banding fowl. Despite the myth, he was far from the first person to band birds. By 1909, bird-banding had become so widespread in the United States that the American Bird Banding Association was formed. He *was*, arguably, the first person, in his own words, to "fill the whole room with heavenly bread right from God's own oven of love" and make himself in the process "twice as famous." This fame was based on the Biblical verse that Jack stamped on one side of the band. The first banded goose to be shot bore the scripture, *Have Faith in God*. According to Jack, when the shooter read that tag to his friends on a street corner in the southern United States, "they had the effect of a real benediction ... and a hush fell." The "miracle" of Wild Goose Jack had begun in earnest.

Soon some very wealthy people became intrigued. The beginning days of wildlife conservation were led by such men; millionaire hunters hoping to protect their sport. American president Theodore Roosevelt was one of them. The great industrialist Henry Ford was also piqued, and loaned Jack his personal cinematographer, Ed Flickenger, who filmed Jack Miner's sanctuary, providing Jack with footage that he used during his later lecture tours. Conceivably, Jack Miner was the first lecturer in North America to incorporate the powerful new medium of film into his talks. These talks he gave are said to have changed the English-speaking world's attitude toward nature.

Strangely, neither the tapes nor the transcripts of Jack's lectures exist anymore and we have only the word of the Jack Miner Foundation as to how significant these talks really were. We know that "Uncle Jack," as he called himself, sometimes broke into song, leading the audience in spirited versions of "Pack Up Your Troubles in Your Old Kit Bag." He told anti-Semitic "Icky and Jakie" stories: "Mister I don't look like so much, but I make lots ... my cheque is good for seventy-five thousand." He made jokes about "Injun Joe and his squaw." "Everybody think like me," he mocked. "Everybody want my squaw." On stage, dressed in his signature red plaid, trousers tucked into thigh high hunting boots, he embodied the perfect country bumpkin, pandering to the racial assumptions of his age, and merging an extremely white-skinned interpretation of nature with what he was pleased to call Methodism.

Armed with professional film footage financed by one of the richest men in the world, and spouting his "Minerisms," as they came to be called, Jack Miner took to the lecture tour with military precision. A standardized information sheet was printed up and mass-mailed to prospective sponsors. It was a no-nonsense document: "I have 2,000 feet of motion pictures ... you supply the machine. MACHINE MUST BE STANDARD SIZE!" This was followed by the now-familiar Jack Miner personality: a false and loud humility combined with 100 percent pure flapdoodle: "As to my personality I am just a grown up boy who was born bare-footed and raised on the toe of father's boot; now grown out of the pink and into the silver-tip class with all to be thankful for and nothing to boast of ... I am still carrying a hundred pounds of steam and no damper."

He performed as many as five times a day for forty days in a row, operating the first .35 mm projector in Canada and accompanied everywhere by a film technician who doubled as a chauffeur. When he lectured to children in the afternoon, he urged them to bring their parents in the evening. His apologists imply that Jack did not charge admission to children, but his posters state emphatically "Children 10 cents (rush 25 cents)." His son, Manly, softened up potential audiences with some aggressive frontwork. "A week ahead I advised the [sponsoring group] to have the mayor meet the train and have a band out. They did all this plus having the Prime Minister of the Province

which resulted in the press giving the occasion front page pub-
licity." By his own account Manly had one thousand community
newspapers on his mailing list.

There was simply no stopping the great Jack Miner. He began
to write books, or at least dictate them to Manly. These books,
often self-published and sold by mail order to maximize profit,
have been conveniently overlooked by gushing commentators of
the Jack Miner story. Vain, eccentric, and idiomatic, they contain such enlightening chapters as "Weasels, and How to Destroy
Them," "Some Things I Have Known Cannibal Birds to Do," and
"Duck's Love Soon Ceases." Included in one is a blueprint of the
"Jack Miner Crow Trap," for those readers who want to help Jack
eradicate that "black, cold-blooded highway murderer" — the
crow. Jack's literary output consists of two books, bewilderingly
rearranged, republished, and resold under different titles, two
of them published well after his death in an apparent attempt
to revive the flagging phenomenon of Wild Goose Jack. Some
of these editions contain so many typographical errors that it
is difficult not to suspect they have been deliberately inserted,
fostering the unlettered-country-boy element of Jack's reputation and underscoring his deep contempt for "book lerning" (his
spelling). As for the writing, it is perhaps enough to say that when
he is not occupied with complimenting himself, Jack attempts to
give the reader "a taste" of what the woods "smell like."

It was not Jack's leaden books alone that brought him his
baffling celebrity. According to Jack every time a banded bird
was shot, the story was picked up by one thousand newspapers
(he does not say if these are the same thousand newspapers that
appeared on his son's mailing list). Accolade was heaped upon
accolade, interviews took place, meetings with great personages
were arranged, radio talks were given. The Uncle Jack mythology
was being created.

With this new and growing stature, Jack Miner became nearly untouchable. If the Canadian government suggested or even begged him to put something other than scripture on his famous bands, the *sex* of the goose for example, or its weight, or approximate age, Jack would laugh their city-bred ignorance right out of the room. The "father of conservation" would have no truck with science.

In the early twenties, when Canadian and United States governments issued identical, numbered bands to naturalists in an effort to correlate bird-banding information, Jack Miner contemptuously dismissed the enterprise and refused to participate. His own scripture-stamped bands were bringing him constant attention from the press and he had no interest in sharing that fame. "You young whipersnappers," he wrote, "just out of college … who sit in your offices and tell me how it should be done!" He viewed the 1925 Scopes "Monkey Trial," allowing evolution to be taught in American schools, as a disgusting perversion. "Apeism," he called it to his dying day, and it meant as little to him as what he liked to call "the price of pork grease in Jerusalem."

Today it is almost impossible to discern what exactly it was that Jack Miner *did*. Both the Grolier and Hurtig Canadian encyclopedia refer to him as a naturalist or a "noted naturalist," although the majority of Jack's observations on nature are not only incorrect, they border on lunacy. The sole reason the moose possesses antlers, he insisted, was because God deliberately put them there to protect the female from the un-Christian "crazed" and "ravishing sexual desire" of the bull. According to Jack the horns of the male get tangled in the bush, allowing the female to run away. Invariably it is the sexual monogamy of animals that decide where they stand on the Jack Miner hierarchy. "I believe every man has the right to take two women," he often joked, "provided one of them is his mother-in-law." He referred to his own wife as "my mother-in-law's daughter."

This lecture-circuit humour reveals a very serious clue to Jack's interpretation of the animal kingdom. The skunk was not monogamous and therefore should be exterminated. The passenger pigeon should also be exterminated, and was, in fact, by God himself. Jack, to the end, insisted the extinction of the passenger pigeon had nothing do with netting or hunting, but was an act of divine providence. God, presumably disgusted by the sexual antics of the creature, reached down from heaven and smote it from the face of the earth. "Yes I want the world to know that I have sound reasons for saying that the gun did not exterminate the passenger pigeon, but that it was the power of Almighty God."

The goose, the duck, and the songbirds, protected by their Christian monogamy, occupied the top echelon of Jack Miner's decidedly peculiar nature fantasy. "The Canada goose is eternally loyal to its mate, setting a noble example for us to follow," he wrote. "When in captivity he will wash himself up and keep clean and respectable and, in about three years, with his mate, will settle down to raise a family of from four to eight, as all Canadians should." In the end, his "practical naturalism" is a Freudian's delight, fraught with sexual fear, inadvertent references to mother-love, and the symbolic manifestation of the goose as the great mother herself. Of course, in the Jack Miner universe, any animal that dared to attack a songbird or a goose, "my pets," he called them, required ruthless extermination. The timber wolf was also a prime target and he urged the people of Ontario "to work harmoniously together and beat the wolf to death."

In 1930, a sixty-five-year-old man, Uncle Jack shot sixty hawks and packed them off to the zoology department of the Royal Ontario Museum to have their stomach contents analyzed.

Most of the species were known to feed on small birds and Jack was hopeful that his overwhelming evidence would lead to a legalized extinction of hawks. He sent out a press release to that effect. In case the "armchair theorists" at the museum missed the point, he jammed a meadow lark down the throat of one of his specimens. Unfortunately for Jack, even the most junior armchair theorist knew that a hawk ripped its prey into small pieces before consuming it. The only person who didn't know, it seems, was Jack Miner.

A nature poet penned "A Rebuke to Jack Miner." Scientists and non-professionals alike were outraged. The New Jersey Audubon Society warned of "the deplorable danger," posed by "a lopsided conservationist." None of this had any effect on the popularity of Jack Miner. The father of conservation scoffed at what he called "armchair naturalists" and quoted scripture at them. The provincial government, fearful of Jack's immense popularity, scrapped its own statute, which, until then, had restricted the shooting of hawks and owls.

In the formidable opinion of Wild Goose Jack, the "heartless and murderous" owl, "the baby murder[ing]" crow, all other "cannibal birds," the wolf, the weasel and the muskrat needed to be wiped from the face of the earth to make way for a new order, ushered in by Jack Miner and his non-adulterous winged messengers of God. It was on the wings of these messengers that Uncle Jack is credited with Christianizing the Indian and the "Eskimo." According to the *Saturday Evening Post*, whenever a Native hunter shot a banded bird, he brought the band to the local missionary and asked, "What has God said this time?" Uncle Jack, an amateur painter of "brightly coloured Bible scenes," would trade one of his paintings in exchange for a returned band. This method of spreading the gospel was said to be so effective that by 1944, at least according to the *Post*, "there's hardly an igloo in these Northern wilds whose interior isn't decorated with some of Jack's scenes." Forty years later, CBC Enterprises published a book that confidently insisted that Jack's banded geese caused Native communities to "explode in a rebirth of religious fervour" producing finally, "the greatest religious revival that missionaries had seen in 30 years."

This type of gullible and reverential language clouds nearly all writings about Jack Miner. Somehow, in the presence of the Uncle Jack phenomenon, even seasoned reporters set aside their skepticism and were reduced to a quasi-religious mumbo jumbo that turned Jack into a visible incarnation of God himself: white-haired, grandfatherly, tall, severe, and all-knowing, with his arms spread out in front of him. Jack, it turns out, did not just feed shell corn to geese, "he ministered to their needs." "There he stands," observes one writer, "true, clean and wholesome." Jack Miner, we are assured, "has opened doors to wonders that are beyond believing."

Given the portrayal of Jack Miner as a saintly being, it is not surprising that he has been credited with single-handedly bringing Christianity to the inhabitants of the far North. While this claim may have comforted his admirers, it in no way manages to hide his contempt for the Native peoples of Canada. "Indians or half breeds and their squaws," he wrote, were "the most inhumane" slaughterers of the beaver, that he had ever seen. "I have only killed 72 beavers in my whole life," he brags, weirdly. He then goes on to say, "I have never heard one Indian even hint at conserving anything … Nothing can be done for the Indian … unless you control the Indian." These inhumane slaughterers were abetted by what Jack called "the drowsy-looking Jew" fur buyer.

The Indian and the Jew working together to wipe out the wild animals of North America — it is a conspiracy that forms the shadowy backdrop of Jack's message, and may explain at least some of his popularity in the press.

Today it seems painfully clear that the Jack Miner story was built on a foundation of contempt. Included in it was anyone with a formal education or a coolness toward hunting. It took in the government, scientists, experts, specialists, and schoolteachers. Reading, writing, science, medicine, botany, geography, any form of study beyond the Bible and back issues of *Rod & Gun* was a waste of time. In the vernacular of Jack Miner and the newspapermen who vaulted him to stardom, there were no scientists, only "so-called scientists," "so-called experts," and "university men," a term that dripped with contempt. Jack Miner, we are told by the *Toronto Daily Star*, "did more to protect wildlife than all the *school room* advice which was given in the same period."

"The greatest *practical* naturalist on the planet," crowed the *Saturday Evening Post*. College would have left him "cribbed, cabined and confined." The code is obvious and expresses the era's reverence for the self-made man and the rugged individualist. As for those lowly "so-called experts" quietly gathering data on the habits of wildlife in an attempt to formulate responsible game-law policy, they were dismissed and ridiculed in the face of the unquestioned anecdotes of the great Jack Miner.

In 1931, the Jack Miner Migratory Bird Sanctuary was incorporated by a special act of the province of Ontario and would stay open in perpetuity as a "permanent memorial to Jack Miner." In a promotional flyer, the Miners described the site as "this one place on earth where no money will ever change hands." The same flyer urged readers to "Make All Cheques Payable and Send To: The Jack Miner Foundation," and closed with a plea to keep the Foundation in mind "When Making Your Will." It was at this sanctuary, critics say, that Jack Miner, by domesticating geese from their natural wariness, caused the death of more geese than he ever possibly saved. As early as 1916, Indians in the James Bay area reported geese banded with scripture, tamer than the rest, coming down to meet decoys where the remaining flock would not. A Hudson's Bay company factor wrote to Jack explaining that "birds that have recourse to your sanctuary ... fall very easy victims to gunners." It was also at his much-publicized sanctuary that Jack kept wild geese in pens, allowing visitors to experience what one writer called, the "privilege of releasing them."

In 1947, the federal government set aside the week of April 10, Jack's birthday, to commemorate National Wildlife Week. Nearly two decades later, Manly Miner, in a prose style that suggests he had more to do with his father's books than just taking dictation, informed the Canadian Tourist Association that he was "not speaking boastfully but it is through the contact I have kept with the press that has helped *put* National Wildlife Week *over* ... It is father's name and fame that has *put* National Wildlife Week *over*." The choice of words is revealing and describes exactly what Jack Miner did. He "put one over" on just about everyone. By 1950, the sanctuary lagged only behind the Dionne Quintuplets and Niagara Falls as the most popular Canadian destination for American tourists. Promotional literature states that, at its height, ten thousand cars a day passed through.

That height has long passed — on a spring day several years ago I was the only visitor in attendance. Today the Jack Miner Migratory Bird Foundation Inc. is still banding birds with scripture. In 1999, 306 newly banded Canada Geese were flying the skyways of North America with an aluminum tag attached to them that read, "Cast All Your Care upon God." These bands, "unique and highly prized by collectors," can be ordered off the www.*jackminer.com* website for twenty-five dollars each.

* * *

Like the moose that he once caricaturized as a sex-crazed animal, Jack Miner himself became a caricature and crackpot, spokesman for millionaire big-game hunters, and a tireless self-promoter with a burning need to glorify himself and his views. By his own admission, he never read a book. He thought history a waste of time and wanted it abolished. He had a habit of calling Canada "America." Like many turn-of-the-century Canadians, he watched his children die of fever, he saw his loved ones and relatives destroyed by alcohol or shot dead in hunting accidents. He hunted raccoons, made stew out of squirrels, and lived on potatoes. As a grown man, he inscribed Scripture on aluminum bands and attached them to the legs of terrified ducks and wild geese. He became famous and was awarded the Order of the British Empire by King George VI. It has been said that "he loved nothing more than to see a hawk or owl dying slowly hanging upside on one of his pole traps." In his own words, he was "brought up by God from a barefoot underprivileged boy to be a man respected by millions." A contemporary and acquaintance, John Jasperson, probably got it right when he said of the man "he was a preacher … he was a salesman, he was a huckster."

Jack Miner died at home in Kingsville, Ontario, in 1944 at the age of seventy-six. His coffin was laid to rest in a wagon-load of soil transported north from his native state of Ohio.

17

Grey Owl:
Round Hole in a Round Peg

Although the world would come to call him Grey Owl, he was born Archibald Stansfeld Furmage into a complicated family. His father, an alcoholic womanizer, big-game hunter, and bankrupted tea-taster, squandered the family's fortune, impregnated a fifteen-year-old girl and disappeared. He later surfaced, supposedly married to an Elizabeth Cox, and, with her and her young sister, sailed for Florida to engage in a disastrous real-estate speculation. He abandoned the pregnant Miss Cox in Florida and returned to England married to her fifteen-year-old pregnant sister.

The child of that pregnancy was born on September 18, 1888, at Hastings. It is doubtful the infant ever saw his father, who showed up intoxicated in Brandon, Manitoba, and was later murdered in a drunken brawl in the United States.

Taken from his child-mother by two maiden aunts, he was given the family name of Belaney. The boy kept a menagerie, was bit by a pet adder, and nearly died. He played constantly at "Red Indian" and claimed he could get within two inches of a bird and not be seen. He built a wigwam in an English garden. At thirteen, to impress a girl, he demonstrated an Indian war dance and fed frogs to his pet snake. He saw his first Indian in 1903 when Buffalo Bill Cody's Wild West Show performed in Hastings. He left school at sixteen, worked in a lumberyard and spent his weekends throwing knives. One afternoon he attempted to topple a statue onto his aunt as she read the newspaper. Later he lowered a homemade bomb down the chimney of his employer's factory. On March 29, 1906, eighteen-year-old Archie Belaney boarded the SS *Canada* bound for Halifax.

Three months later, he squatted in a canoe in the Temagami district of Ontario. Taken on as a chore boy at a local inn, he carried a notebook to jot down Indian words. In 1907, he returned to England to scrounge funds. His footwear now consisted only of moccasins. Friends described him walking the streets of Hastings "with the loping gait of an Indian." While there he learned of his father's death in America.

By summer's end he was back as chore boy at the Temagami Inn. With his father out of the way, he gave himself a new history, growing up an Indian in the American Southwest, son of a Scot trader and full-blooded Apache girl. In broken Ojibwa, sign language, and a few words of English, he romanced an Indian girl, Angele, and through her befriended Ned White Bear, who wore an alarm clock under his shirt. He mastered more than two hundred words of Ojibwa and learned to put the verb before the noun. About this time he was given the name *ko-home-see* (little owl) by one of Angele's uncles who called him, "the little owl who sits taking in everything."

On August 23, 1910, he married Angele in a civil service in a fire ranger's hall on Bear Island. A local Ojibway played violin. He later told his wife, teasingly, that he would make a white woman of her. "No Archie," she said. "I make Indian of you." (Forty years later Angele explained to a reporter: "Maybe he not always tell the truth. But he a good man, my man.")

In 1911, he fathered a child. The girl's baptismal certificate provides the first documentary proof of Archie's existence in Canada, recording his name as Arthur Belenge. Echoing the father he never met, he abandoned Angele and his infant daughter. In 1912, he walked from Temagami to Toronto, the same year he made his first appearance in the village of Biscotasing. Employed as a fire ranger, he received monthly cheques from his aunts, mailed small sums to Angele, but never included a note.

In 1912, Biscotasing was a village of summering Indians, French Canadian timbermen, and Scots and English traders. The village's white Protestants received sermons from an Ojibway minister. Here Archie Belaney established himself as "a white man with possibly a streak of Indian in him." His skin was dark from the sun, his long hair kept out of his eyes by two loops of fishing line. By now he was telling people his father died violently while employed as a Texas Ranger. He himself, he said, fought the Yaqui Indians in Mexico.

He surfaced in Montreal in 1913, but immediately returned to Biscotasing. There, at his rooming house, he met Marie Girard, a young Métis woman who spoke fluent French, English, and Ojibwa, and had never spent a day in school. He invited her to join him on his trapline. In 1914, across a campfire, he asked a student from the University of Toronto, "Do you think I could write?" He continued to modify his family history; his father, a Texas Ranger, was now murdered by a Mexican, who, in turn, was killed by Archie. In a masterstroke, he claimed to have been a young member of Buffalo Bill's Wild West Show, through which he met his father's sisters who raised him for a time "near London." This helped explain his curious English accent. By now he was drinking heavily and writing on sheets of foolscap. In 1914, after returning from the Goulais River country, he got drunk and demolished his rooming-house. Before he could be arrested, he escaped into the bush with Marie Girard, who was pregnant with his child.

The next verifiable sighting of Archie Belaney occurred May 6, 1915, half a continent away at Digby, Nova Scotia, where he enlisted in the Canadian Army. He gave his birthplace as Montreal, his marital status as single, and claimed previous military experience in the 28th Mexican Dragoons. In 1915, stationed in England, he went AWOL to visit his aunts. Unknown to him, Marie Girard had given birth to his son and died soon after of tuberculosis. Joined to the 13th Battalion of the Royal Highlanders, Belaney saw action in France as a sniper. A fellow soldier noticed him "squirm up muddy hills in a way no white man could."

In January 1916, he took a bullet to the wrist and was hospitalized for two weeks. A bullet smashed his right foot in April, and he would be unable to walk properly for the rest of his life. In 1917, at the London General Hospital, his fourth metatarsus and fourth toe were removed. There he met and later corresponded with a young nurse. "He spoke English very badly," she said. "His spelling was simply awful. No educated Englishman could spell so badly."

It now appears that Archie Belaney was attempting to translate ten thousand years of oral tradition into the voice of an Indian literary narrative:

"Gee Im lucky to be able to travel the big woods agen. To us peple the woods and the big hills and the Northern lights and the sunsets are all alive and we live with these things and live in the spirit of the woods like no white person can do ... I wonder if all this means anything to you I hope you wont laugh at it anyway."

The limping twenty-five-year-old was laying down the pidgin Injun dialect that Hollywood talkies would soon eagerly emulate. He was also taking the first tentative stabs at an indigenous literary form, free of European sophistication and American muscle, hinting at an honesty that would make him, briefly, one of the most popular writers and lecturers in the English-speaking world.

While convalescing in Hastings, Archie reintroduced himself to a childhood sweetheart, Ivy Holmes, now twenty-six. In February, 1917 at Hollington Church-in-the-Wood, he married her. According to the unsuspecting young bride: "he had a way making the backwoods sound very attractive ..."

II

Things did not go well for Archie Belaney following his discharge from the army. Back in Biscotasing, he learned Marie Girard was dead and that he now had a second child, a son. The boy, Johnny, was raised by his former rooming-house landlady, Edith Langevin, a Cree midwife said to have delivered every child in Biscotasing. The boy referred to his father as Archie Baloney. Having kept his British wife waiting for nearly two years, he wrote her a letter confessing his marriage to Angele. She promptly divorced him as a bigamist. Archie drank hard again and was seen stirring his homemade mash with a canoe paddle. He got drunk on shoe polish.

Still an excellent canoeist, in 1920–21 he found a job as a deputy ranger on the Mississauga Forest Reserve. There he composed his first public statement as a conservationist — copied on a piece of birchbark and nailed to a tree: "God made this country for the trees — Don't burn it up and make it look like hell." He rejected the theory of evolution on the grounds that, "Monkeys didn't drink, beat up their wives, and leave." During this time he got to know a little girl named Libby who would later call him "one of the nicest things that happened to me when

I was growing up." For a number of years he was befriended by an Ojibwa family, the Espaniels, to whom he attributed "calm & quiet contentment, little intimate enjoyments" and "the appreciation of the woods in its fullest sense." Later he would inscribe a book to Mr. Espaniel: "To one whom I am proud to call Dad."

By now he was filling his knapsacks with notes and writing stories. He walked compulsively through the bush at night to avoid what he called "the abyss of introspection." In his own words he had become "a human distillery." He began to dye his hair black and redden his skin with henna. Reportedly he rolled a spoon back and forth across his nose to flatten it. He invented a war dance, probably from readings in Longfellow and James Fenimore Cooper. He sang Indian war songs that neither the Cree nor Ojibwa understood. He beat on a war drum made from a cheese box. With a warrant out for his arrest for "unlawfully conducting himself in a disorderly manner whilst drunk at the Biscotasing Railway Station," he left "Bisco" and returned to Temagami.

Working as a guide there in 1925, he stayed with his first wife, Angele. Within a year he had a second daughter by her. In the fall, the first daughter, Agnes, now fourteen, saw her father off at the train station. He told her, "I go away. I will come back sometime. I like travel." She never saw him again.

Concerned by the near extinction of the beaver, in 1925, the Ontario government banned non-Indians from fur trapping. Despite his henna and war dances, Archie Belaney was very officially not an Indian and moved to northern Quebec to maintain his livelihood. In 1926, he enclosed a photograph in a letter sent to his Hastings aunts. "This is my wife Gertie, an Iroquois chief's daughter, twenty-one years old..." He had met the girl as a nineteen-year-old waitress at a camp. He was smitten by her and she in turn would write two books about him as "Anahareo," the name that Archie would later give her. (He also tenderly called her "Insect.".). The young woman soon learned her lover could not stand an argument and suffered from a weak heart. In the summer of 1926, an Indian chief pronounced them man and wife. She worked a trapline with him, and, sickened by the killing of the animals, solidified in Archie a belief that the death of the beaver meant the death of the woods.

In 1928 the two moved to Cabano on the New Brunswick border, taking two pet beavers with them. There Archie Belaney set his traps for the last time. With no income except a small military pension, he homesteaded in a squatter's shack with the hope of establishing a beaver colony. Having little else to do, he wrote an essay in praise of the white trapper, published by the British magazine *Country Life*, who requested a book. By 1930, he had developed a taste for vanilla extract, for drinking, not baking, and wore a bottle of it on a string around his neck. It was reported to a priest that he drank turpentine. At the village of Métis he was reduced to selling ten-cent admissions to see his pet beaver. In the same village, he delivered his first lecture on the wilderness at a tourist hotel. It was well received and earned him fifteen dollars. He became known as the "beaver man" and was approached by local scoutmasters wanting him to teach lessons on bush craft.

His relationship to his pet beavers not only contributed to his eventual status as a world-famous lecturer, they also transformed him from a mediocre trapper into a committed conservationist with a genuine feeling for wildlife. He came to recognize the zoo as the "saddest place in any city," and he let people know it. Contained in his love of the wild was a potent anger toward people. "Man," he claimed, "was the parasite supreme of all the earth." He believed the wilderness "was a living, breathing reality with a soul" and that all living things in the forest had a right to live. Not only did he believe these things, but he went public with them. He trumpeted a message that the world had never heard before, at a time when even the forestry branch of the Canadian government thought nothing of sowing the forest floor with strychnine pellets dropped from aircraft.

Very quickly, a nascent conservation movement converged around Archie Belaney. A short film about him, one of many, was made by officials of the Parks Board. He was invited to address the national convention of the Canadian Forestry Association in Montreal. Following the lecture, he was approached by an elderly gentleman who shook his hand and said tellingly, "I don't know whether I have just heard a poem or an encyclopedia on wildlife." The next day a Montreal paper ran the headline "Full Blooded Indian Gives Lecture on Wildlife." His wife, Anahareo, later noted that the more he wrote, the more Indian he became in the eyes of the public. In 1931, the most visible symbol of wilderness protection in Canada, he was offered the post of caretaker at Riding Mountain National Park in Manitoba, and given the opportunity to successfully establish a beaver colony.

His first book, *Men of the Last Frontier*, was published later that year under the name of Grey Owl. The original manuscript showed the teeth marks of a beaver that tried to make a bed out of it. According to the *Times Literary Supplement*, it was "difficult to recall any record of the Great North so brilliantly and lovingly handled."

"Grey Owl is no stuffed Indian," said the *New York Times*. A year later, the book appeared in Canadian school readers. Only one critic argued it must have been ghost-written since "no half breed trapper could pick up such an elegant style."

He lived in a small shack in Prince Albert National Park with an active beaver lodge in his living room. In the summer of 1932, his wife gave birth to a daughter. Prior to the birth, Anahareo, who had not put on a dress in six years, desperately demanded to know what size maternity dress she should order. Equally desperate, Archie told his 110-pound wife "Get the biggest they've got!" He worked on a second book. His wife, who sometimes dressed their infant in a rabbit robe she'd won off a Hudson's Bay factor in a poker game, placed the child with a woman friend in Prince Albert, and, to her husband's envy, took off to prospect a mining field on the banks of the Churchill River. "Keep a spare paddle," he told her. "And never run too stern heavy. Use the portage if there is any doubt at all. It is not so glorified but it is better than a post mortem."

Eager for American rights to his books, he told Scribner's editor Max Perkins, "I am an American myself & proud of it." His second book, *Pilgrims of the Wild*, sold fifty thousand copies in the U.K. alone. At Max Perkins's request, he wrote a children's book, *The Adventures of Sajo and Her Beaver People*. It has since been translated into eighteen languages. The prose, softly humorous, excels in his characteristic personification of animals: "I am afraid that their table manners were not very nice, as there was a good deal of rather loud smacking of lips and hard breathing to be heard, and they often talked with their mouths full." He also displays a full respect for the linguistic capabilities of children, remaining free of the patronizing, crushing simplicity that defines the genre today. Of young Sajo's beavers he writes:

> The larger one of the two was called Chilawee, or Big Small, and the not-so-large one was called Chikanee, or Little Small. Unfortunately they did not grow evenly; that is, one would grow a little faster than the other for a while, and then he would slack down and the other would catch up, and get ahead of him. First one was bigger than the other, then the other was

bigger than the one! And it would be discovered that
Little Small had been Big Small for quite some time,
whilst Big Small had been going around disguised as
Little Small ... It was all very confusing and Sajo had
just about decided to give them one name between
them and call them just "The Smalls."

In 1935 he undertook a gruelling British tour, lecturing
three and four times a day to crowds so large that police were
called in to control them. "I am Grey Owl," he began. "I come
from across the seas to tell you about my Canadian homeland."
He was called the best writer on animals "in any language." His
books were selling at the rate of two thousand a week. His British
publisher, Lovat Dickson, a Canadian, wrote his biography and
for the next forty years refused to believe the man was anything
but a Mexican-born half-Apache.

After four months and some three hundred lecture dates, he
sailed for home. On board he drank heavily, ate only onions, and
was noticeably ill. Off the shores of Halifax, he resumed regular
meals and began work on *Tales of an Empty Cabin*. Arriving in
Toronto, he made an unflattering comment about the value of
organized religion to the Indian and was vilified by the press.
In Ottawa, he had dinner with the prime minister. He was photographed by Karsh. Back in Prince Albert, his wife attempted
to strangle him and then fled for California. By now his health
was so broken that he could barely carry a pail of water. Despite
that, he made it to Montreal where he married a woman named
Yvonne Perrier and inexplicably signed his name Archie McNeil.
There is no doubt that when he wanted to, Archie could be a
determined suitor; in the early days of their romance he wrote a
letter to Anahareo that spanned 104 pages. Archie and his new
wife took the train back to Prince Albert with the bride watching

her husband drink himself to sleep. In Prince Albert he was too weak to carry a pack.

Abruptly he sailed with his wife to Buckingham Palace, where he gave a private lecture to the Royal Family. He started another British tour, having barely survived the first one. This one took him 4,300 miles. He gave 130 lectures. He was seen swallowing white pills by the handful. When it was over, the BBC refused to broadcast his farewell speech, as it contained a reference to fox hunting. Bitterly disappointed over this, and sick, he boarded the SS *Berengaria* for North America. He spent the next three months touring the United States and Canada. Living on raw eggs and whiskey, he returned to his cabin in Prince Albert and died there in April, 1938, two months short of his fiftieth birthday.

III

In his brief life, Archie Belaney conquered the great distances of his adopted country. By boat, by train, by canoe, by foot, by snowshoe, he was constantly moving. From the city to the bush and back again, across the ocean and back again. He was always on the move, always searching for a native place in which to live, and to hide. From Charles Dickens to Franz Kafka and Graham Greene, he personified Europe's fascination with the "Red Indian." Not content to be fascinated, he attempted to *become*. Eventually he became the most famous Red Indian in the world. We are told that his speech, (the phoniest, cringe-making "heap-em Big Chief" accent imaginable complete with bogus hand gestures) revealed "the true nasal twang of the Canadian Indian." He became the blue-eyed Indian the world wanted. Not hunched over a stack of law books in Osgoode Hall, memorizing the British North America Act, but on stage, whooping it up in a war dance, and petting a beaver, the animal he once slaughtered and then almost single-handedly saved from extinction. He insisted the true custodians of the wilderness were Indians. He met kings and prime ministers and begged them to put Indians in charge of the forest. According to John Diefenbaker, he was the greatest conservationist that this nation has ever produced. "Like all great men," said Diefenbaker, "he had his warts."

As a child, Archie Belaney knew that a secret waited for him in the forests of Canada. He came in search of it and in his own lifetime saw those forests disappear for good. He became the world's leading spokesman of the "calm and silent presence of the trees ... the trust and confidence of small animals ... Without that," he wrote, "I am nothing." He saw the dams and the strip mines ripping into the land that he came to love. He wrote and worked himself to death in passionate devotion to keep that land alive. "I will stand on my head," he told Anahareo, "if it will make people listen." In attempting to start a new life Archie Belaney dramatically rejected the old one; the world of Europe hell-bound for war and suffocated by machines and tyranny. "Call me Grey Owl," he said. Archibald was a "high-sounding preten-tious, cake-eating epithet, just Grey Owl, please."

The transformation of Archie Belaney into an Apache half-breed is the story of a man who, for a moment, spanned the two great solitudes of North America. He was both immigrant and native. He went native, not by accident but on purpose, know-ing it was essential for him. He was civilized and "savage," north and south at the same time. In the course of this extraordinary balancing act, he became something that never existed before.

Today, in some photographs, he looks slightly pathetic in a full Indian headdress bought from a souvenir shop in London, England. He looks gaunt and gravely ill. He is gravely ill. But in other pictures, entertaining an Ojibway boy confined to the

Peterborough Hospital, or photographed from the waist up, paddling a canoe on a wild river, he appears triumphant, a smile of pure contentment on his handsome face. In this moment, he is the most successful imposter, the man who apparently in all honesty told a reporter, "I'm just a round peg in a round hole."

18

Charles Bedaux:
Lost in the Mountains

On May 25, 1934, with his wife, his mistress, and maid at his side, Charles Bedaux, a French-born naturalized American millionaire, announced to an assembly of Canadian officials that he was about to undertake an overland trek through the Rocky Mountains to the Pacific Ocean, a journey that had not been attempted since Alexander Mackenzie in 1793.

This trip, "the Bedaux Sub-Arctic Expedition," has been called "one of the strangest expeditions in the history of modern exploration," and centred on a wild scheme to drive six Citröen half-tracks through some of the most rugged terrain in the world. It was, in its conception, an attempt to cross the Rocky Mountains by tractor.

Accompanying Bedaux on his expedition was an Italian countess thought to be his mistress, an Academy Award–winning Hollywood cameraman, a Swiss skiing instructor, a host of wranglers, cowboys, a dental student, an unemployed bush pilot, guides, geologists, and a British Columbia provincial surveyor. Their aim was to traverse not only the Rockies, but the Stikine Mountains, an 1,100-mile journey, half of it through roadless and unknown territory, using five cream-coloured, nickel-plated Citröen half-track trucks imported from France; all-terrain trucks with wheels in front and caterpillar tracks in the back, built by Andre Citröen, an acquaintance of Bedaux's. The trucks were backed up by an estimated one hundred pack horses.

On July 6, following a champagne breakfast at Edmonton's Hotel Macdonald, and a hearty send-off by the lieutenant governor, the party, including at that point two limousines, set out in the pouring rain on the first leg of the journey; a five-hundred-mile jaunt across the mud roads to Fort St. John.

Within three weeks they had passed through Athabasca, Grande Prairie, Dawson Creek, and eventually cut north to Montney, the last outpost on a crude trail cut by Depression relief gangs. They were literally at the end of the road. The following day saw the six Citröens hauled by block and tackle three hundred yards through a swamp. The expedition, at this point, was making one hundred yards an hour and Bedaux's team was forced to construct corduroy roads to move forward at all.

Thirty-nine miles out from Fort St. John, Bedaux fired his radio operator, an act that later commentators have denounced as irresponsible, if not criminal, since it meant that the provincial surveyor could no longer get a fix on a Greenwich time signal. According to Bedaux, however, the only information the operator was ever able to get from the radio was that the gangster John Dillinger had been shot dead.

With July coming to an end, Bedaux realized that his famed state-of-the-art Citröens, were in fact, useless in the mountains; even on the best of days they managed only twelve miles an hour and consumed massive amounts of fuel in the process. He arranged for several of the machines to be dramatically destroyed, the event being filmed by Floyd Crosby, the resident filmmaker who would go on to make his fame with *High Noon*.

One of the now-useless caterpillar cars was mounted on a raft and floated down river with the intention of having it drift into a cliff, previously rigged with dynamite. The dynamite turned out to be a dud and the Citröen, instead of blowing up into filmic smithereens, floated down river intact, finally washed up on shore and was salvaged by a local rancher who managed to get another thirty years of service from it. Another of the abandoned trucks ended up in the Western Development Museum in Moose Jaw, where it remains today.

By now, the slightly insane foundations of the undertaking were beginning to expose themselves. With the vehicles gone, the much-publicized Beduax Sub-Arctic Expedition consisted of some hundred pack horses, all of which on August, 4, dramatically entered the glacial water of the Halfway River, a scene that has perhaps never been witnessed again by anyone outside of a Hollywood movie set. It was not a trip that lacked grandiosity. The party had reached unmapped territory and the provincial surveyor, Frank Swannell, in his official capacity, promptly named a mountain after Bedaux, and a lake, Lake Fern, after his wife. On September 8, they forded the Kwadacha River and Bedaux broke out a case of champagne — an act that has outraged nearly all future Canadian commentators. This case quickly evolved into "cases" and is unfailingly trotted out to prove that Bedaux was a fraudulent dilettante city slicker messing about where he didn't belong. One participant would later noted that a case of twelve bottles, one of them broken, was not such a big deal for a veteran, hard-drinking, thirsty crew of twenty-two people.

By the middle of September, the decision was made to begin shooting the horses, most of which were starving and in desperate shape. Morale was not high; a former Royal Navy commander, Reginald Geake, a local hire thought to be a British spy, incurred the wrath of the party when he took an axe and split open the head of a stray dog that had joined the expedition. This odd character would later team up with a blind man who could apparently divine the location of gold and set out on foot into the Sierra Madre, where he was shot dead by bandits. By late September, hoof rot set in among the horses and they were being shot at the rate of two or three a day.

A month later, well short of his Telegraph Creek destination, Bedaux called it quits. Even this he presented as a victory. "I am going to present a report together with the data we gathered to the International Highway Commission," he announced. He also sent a handful of Peace River mud to France to be analyzed by French scientists, an act that led an Edmonton newspaper to run the intriguing headline, "France to Have Gumbo Sample." With the sample of muck on its way, Bedaux disappeared from Canada.

History, to say the least, has not been kind to Charles E. Bedaux. His wild escapade into the mountains has been soundly condemned as a $250,000 publicity stunt, and not even the Alaska Highway, begun eight years later, and following the Bedaux route, has helped to rehabilitate him. He was, according to author Pierre Berton, who never met him, "a hateful man," not even a man, but a "creature," who possessed "all the bad qualities of a self-made millionaire." To Berton he was "a fascist," and a "martinet." He was "chunky," "bullet headed," and, even worse in Berton's view, he was short; "a five-foot-six egoist trying desperately and not very effectively to be noticed."

In fact, Bedaux had been effectively noticed all over the world. By the time he embarked on his disastrous Rocky Mountain trek, he was already known for having single-handedly invented an industrial speed-up or "efficiency" system, which at its peak was being employed throughout North America, Europe, and even the Soviet Union, counting among its more than six hundred clients such giants as General Electric, Campbell Soup, Fiat, Kodak, and many more. This system, which made Bedaux the scourge of labour and the darling of management, has been described as the most completely exhausting "efficiency" system ever invented, and a means of squeezing the last drop of blood out of the worker. In spite of these criticisms, both the American Federation of Labor and the Committee for Industrial Organization were Bedaux clients, and his system was reportedly in use by all AFL operations for more than a decade.

The system, like Bedaux himself, was a weird and sometimes unfathomable mix of practicality and mysticism, and involved the invention (Bedaux called it a "discovery") of a new unit to measure human exertion, called — the Bedaux. The grand aim was to replace the old sixty minutes of the clock labour measurement and establish in its place sixty Bedauxs of work. Bedaux, known to his intimates as "Charles the Man," typically introduced himself with the disconcerting statement, "I am the discoverer of the measurement of human energy." From this odd opening he would launch into a spellbinding, and usually successful, sales pitch.

He was born Charles Eugene Bedaux in Paris, France, 1886. At the age of nineteen and well on his way to becoming another Parisian delinquent, he immigrated to New York City and began his career with the most menial of jobs; a "sand hog," hauling wheelbarrows filled with sand from the banks of the East River, and later washing dishes. From these lowly occupations his rise was meteoric, and often unbelievable. He either sold or invented a toothpaste that was supposedly capable of removing ink stains. By 1916 he had patented a machine for timing the duration of telephone calls and was thought to be working on another that

recorded them. He is said to have invented the boom micro-
phone to prevent the loss of time incurred by people tripping
over wires. He also gave esoteric public lectures, attended by
agents of the War College Division of the U.S. War Department
who came to the conclusion that he was a German spy.

With the burgeoning success of his industrial theories,
he travelled extensively, dispensing money, advice, and wild
schemes. In northern British Columbia he tried to convince
local Natives to transport pitchblende to market — by canoe.
He reportedly brought the first running water to Fort St. John
by constructing a pipeline. Long before he dreamed of motor-
ing across the Rockies by Citröen, he developed and patented
an improved car door. He invented and patented mechanical
toys, and, in a mysterious and almost unbelievable undertaking in 1929, was the first man to traverse the Libyan Desert, an
immense journey that served as a precursor to his Canadian Sub-
Arctic Expedition, this one again by car, ten thousand miles, said
to be "the first ever crossing of Africa by vehicle above the equator at the desert's widest point." He bought a castle in France and
in 1937 invited Wallis Simpson and the former King of England
to get married in it, which they did.

He created, and, at the request of the Vichy government,
implemented in Roquefort, France, a bizarre social experiment
that eliminated money, using instead another Bedaux invention
called the "Bex," a standard and stable unit, at least in Bedaux's
mind, that essentially would eliminate commerce. This bizarre
scheme was the basis of a new Bedaux economic and social phi-
losophy which he called "Equivalism." By this point, Bedaux
had passed light years beyond shaving off a few minutes from
a task on the factory floor; he was envisioning and even trying
to implement a new world order, what he called "a capitalism
within the form of communism."

"I wish to go neither right or left," he stated, "I wish to go forward."

From these quixotic declarations, Charles Bedaux seemed almost blissfully unaware that the world was at war and that he was cuddling up to some odious regimes. He courted the Soviets, the Greeks, the Americans, the French, and the German High Command with equal intensity, becoming in the words of his most severe critics, "a self-appointed, semi-salvationist world organizer." A German sculptress created a bust of Bedaux that was shown in an exhibit along with busts of Hitler and Goering. Then, in yet another typically ambitious frenzy, Bedaux undertook the scheme that would destroy him — an ingenious plan to build a trans-Saharan pipeline for pumping edible peanut oil into German-occupied lands.

As American forces advanced through North Africa, Bedaux was spotted drinking brandy on a terrace with a German officer, and, on December 5, 1944, he was arrested as a collaborator by French forces. As a naturalized American, Bedaux was flown to Miami, where he stood trial for treason. On February 14, days before a verdict was delivered, he swallowed a carefully hoarded overdose of Luminal and killed himself in a room above a garage in the Miami border patrol station. In a cryptic note, Bedaux implied that powerful people made it impossible for him to tell the truth, that he was "a good, honest, deserving American." The note ended with a pledge of everlasting love to his wife.

Although there seems little doubt that Charles Bedaux committed suicide, it was the respected, perhaps overly respected, American journalist, Janet Flanner who definitively buried him.

In an exhaustive three-part series titled "Annals of Collaboration," published in the *New Yorker* several months after his death, she skewers the man as a self-deluded egoist, a braggart, "a Fascist favouring millionaire," who spoke imperfect English, and consorted with "Nazi chums." Not even his lonely death elicits sympathy from Flanner, who coldly describes his suicide note as "a Classic," criticizing even his signature for too much resembling that of a banker's. Bedaux was, she states, wittily enough, "the only American who had ever "sold out his country literally for peanuts."

While the world found it in its heart to forgive Coca-Cola, IBM, Coco Chanel, and many others for collaborating with the Nazis, that same forgiveness has not extended to Charles Bedaux. Flanner's authoritative article closed the book on the strange and troubled life of the one-time sandhog and dishwasher from Paris. Probably it would have remained shut for good if not for the Bedaux Canadian Sub-Arctic Expedition. Although the expedition warrants only a single small paragraph in the Flanner hatchet job, it has, over the years, slowly assumed mythic proportions to Canadian writers who refuse to lose interest in the lore of Charles Bedaux. From *Saturday Night* and *Canadian Geographic*, to *Maclean's*, *Car and Driver Magazine* (which credits Bedaux with inventing off-road racing), Pierre Berton, Jim Christy's 1984 biography *The Price of Power*, and George Ungar's fascinating and award-winning documentary, *The Champagne Safari*, every decade spurs a new Canadian interest in Bedaux's bizarre and failed trek through the Rockies.

Because of these writers and filmmakers, just about every odd detail of the Canadian Sub-Arctic Expedition is now public knowledge, from the Devonshire cream and the candied fruits, to the time it took to conduct Fern Bedaux's morning toilet. Charles Eugene Bedaux, however, remains as inaccessible and remote as ever; a man who was willing to wheel, deal, and socialize with the Nazis, and yet a man who, according to his biographer, may have been peripherally involved in the plot to assassinate Hitler. A greedy millionaire who wanted to eliminate poverty and do away with money altogether; a "fascist" who dreamed of establishing a Jewish homeland in Africa, who started out pushing wheelbarrows in his adopted country and ended up on trial for treason there.

Perhaps one of the few guarded glimpses of the man himself is to be found in an innocuous remark that he made to Canadian reporters during his Rocky Mountain extravaganza: "I work hard," he said. "Between work periods I enjoy doing things that have not been done by others." It is perhaps not surprising that the man the world considered an expert on time and labour, did not do work; he had, instead, "work periods."

He is buried in Mount Auburn Cemetery in Cambridge. His lasting namesake, Mount Bedaux in northern British Columbia, reaches some 7,500 feet into the sky.

19

Selwyn Dewdney:
Touching an Alien Culture

O f all the human ashes "commended" to Lake Superior, perhaps few have settled there as completely and as deservedly
as those belonging to Selwyn Dewdney. In the course of his life,
he was alternately an amateur historian, an amateur writer, an
amateur novelist, a painter (and a good one), an amateur ethnographer, a schoolteacher, a pioneer art therapist, and even
a missionary, of which he would later say, "It sickens me now
to recall how readily I could assume the moral arrogance of
my race."

From a distance it seems that all of these activities served
as an excuse to get himself into the bush, where he became a
consummate professional. He sensed that the Native presence
manifested itself in every significant moment of Canadian life
and, in 1976, three years before his death, he made a startling
statement: "I have come to believe that the impact of aboriginal values and attitudes have shaped us more than we know."
With this quiet observation, he challenges the Canadian grade-
school doctrine that insists on the passive Native, the Native
without agency, driven to near extinction by microbe-ridden

newcomers. It is a radical, empowering observation, and it turns the study of Canadian history on its head.

Selwyn Hanington Dewdney was born in 1909 to the man who would become the second Anglican Bishop of Keewatin, the largest single diocese in the world. He grew up in Prince Albert, Saskatchewan, alongside the Cree families that in his words, "loitered along River Street between Révillon Frères and the Firehall." It was a time when the Révillon Frères stores were as common in Canada as the trading outlets of the Hudson's Bay Company and performed the same function. As a boy, he played not Cowboys and Indians, but "Métis and Mountie," and acted out the Riel Rebellion.

He lived for some time in Kenora, previously known as Rat's Portage, and in 1928, at the age of nineteen, set out with his father on an extraordinary 3,800-mile Episcopal journey to visit the Cree and Ojibway and Chipewayan missions in the far North at Big Trout Lake. His father was sixty-five years old and recovering from a kidney operation. This trip was formative for the young Dewdney and took him into a world that is hardly imaginable. Most of this journey was undertaken by canoe and the canoemen each carried a dog-eared prayer book printed in Cree syllabics; "Bible Cree," Dewdney called them, and they used a syllabic alphabet invented by the missionary James Evans at Norway House in 1841. Evans made his ink out of animal blood.

In order to get to the departure point at Big Trout Lake, it was necessary to drive a gasoline car over the deteriorating Hudson Bay Railway line. Arriving finally at their destination, Selwyn noted a ten-foot fence thrown up around the Hudson's Bay Company vegetable garden. It had been erected in an effort to keep the bears out. The residents of Big Trout Lake, according to Dewdney, had never seen a gas-powered engine of any kind, and they greeted him, "*Wahchee!*" a corruption of a centuries-old British greeting: "What cheer?" In the south, the northwestern brigades had been traditionally greeted with a shout of "*Booshoo!*" — a centuries-old corruption of the French-Canadian greeting, "Bonjour!"

He graduated in 1931 with a Bachelor of Arts degree in astronomy and English from the University of Toronto. During this time as a student, he found occasion to snowshoe down University Avenue. He followed up with an arts degree from the Ontario College of Art, and five years later took a position as high school assistant in London, Ontario, until his resignation in 1946. The circumstances of that resignation would become the subject of his first novel, *Wind without Rain*. In 1936, he married Irene Maude Donner. His father performed the wedding ceremony, and, not surprisingly, his honeymoon consisted of a five-hundred-mile canoe trip. The Peterborough — or what he called the Algonkian — canoe became a type of proxy religion for Dewdney, a wedding vessel; an appendage to his body and the instrument by which he navigated his passage through life. He gave his canoes names, and, when they wrecked, he composed and spoke eulogies over them. "My love for canoes," he wrote, "has the same degree of generality as my affection for women. I do not love them all equally."

His love of northern Ontario, particularly the Lake Superior area, is undeniable and heartfelt and would appear to be the driving force behind much of his work. He spent time in the ghost town of Nicholson, when it still had a pulse, and painted the wooden church there; a church that has long has since collapsed into the earth. When he describes a young Sekani child sucking on a freshly caught trout, his delight is palpable. As a young missionary, he stood on the brink of history, a witness to the last fur brigade coming down from Osnaburgh House, "the trappers paid off at the Hudson's Bay store." This incident encompassed four hundred years of Canadian history and contained in it the birth and the death of a nation built on furs. It is tantalizing to imagine this young man, his eyes wide open, watching the shape of history and nameless trappers, "lying dead drunk along the railway... puking behind the CNR station." Cartier, Radisson, the voyageurs, the canoe brigades of the North West Company — the Hudson's Bay Company; five centuries coming to an end.

Today Selwyn Dewdney is known as *the* pioneering historian of Native rock art of the Canadian Shield. A man who dedicated thirty years of his life to the study of these inscrutable rock painting and the author of *Indian Rock Paintings of the Great Lakes*, a seminal work on Canadian rock art, and just about the only one.

If someone asked Selwyn Dewdney what he did for a living, he answered, "It so happens that I'm the greatest living authority on aboriginal art east of the Rockies." The boast is justified, but it is hollow; the field was his alone. The study of Native rock was almost without provenance or history in Canada, beset by the annual declaration by one Canadian newspaper or another, that Native rock art is really the work of artistic Vikings. Others insist the drawings were put here by aliens from outer space. The meaning of these rock paintings is entirely unknown to us. They have not been dated and Selwyn wrote a dense and informed monograph that outlines the difficulty in doing so. They would seem to predate the arrival of the Ojibway and the Cree, but this is not known with certainty. There are clearly post-contact paintings, a horse, for example, a figure holding a gun. The bonding agent in the paint is thought to be sturgeon oil, perhaps blood, or bear fat, or possibly no bonding agent was used. Ancient trails were used to bring the ochre and down from the hematite mines at Wawa and the substance was widely traded. It seems that the ochre was fried or heated over a fire. No commercial paint has been able to match, or even come close, to the adhesive power of the paint used on the rock faces of the Canadian Shield.

In his vigorous life, Selwyn Dewdney visited and recorded more than three hundred of these sites all over the Canadian Shield. As to their meaning, their purpose, he offers no idea, no way in, and anyone cracking open *Indian Rock Paintings of the Great Lakes* will be disappointed by the book's lack of curiosity, the safety of the observations, and the author's need to appear as some sort of dispassionate scientist. However, the legwork and the knowledge were real. The first and second edition of this book bears a forward by the prime minister of Canada, Leslie Frost, in which he bears tribute to "the vital and salutary benefits derived from union with nature." He was perhaps the first and last head of state to urge "a union with nature." At the very least, this book provided a good excuse for what would seem to be the overriding purpose of Selwyn Dewdney's life: to be in the bush, in or on the water, to sleep outside, to smell the fragrance of pines, and to escape what he called the crushing boredom created by technology and convenience.

He bought himself a Volkswagen van and toured the Great Lakes area in search of rock art. On one of his rock-painting excursions on the Lafayette Peninsula in northern Michigan, he and his wife learned of the existence of nearby rock paintings and hurried off to investigate. They found the paintings, stick men with their maleness indicated by an erect phallus. This detail had so alarmed the manageress of a nearby girls' camp that she had the prehistoric drawings painted over. For Dewdney, she might as well have put a match to the Dead Sea Scrolls and perhaps that is what she had done. He spent four years searching for the extensive displays of rock painting of Mishepishu,

the great horned lynx first described more than a century earlier by American Indian agent and ethnographer Henry Rowe
Schoolcraft. Schoolcraft's massive and compromised legacy of
Native studies led him to conclude that the Native language of
the Ojibway was not Native enough, and this justified his invention of words to help it out. *Algoma* is one example.

Dewdney eventually found these paintings on the Agawa
Rock, nestled deep in the cliff shoreline of Lake Superior Provincial
Park. Today they are heavily visited and require serious contortions on the part of anyone willing to hug a rock face to inspect
them. They look out from the Agawa Rock a few feet above the
churning waters of Lake Superior and depict that monster in all
of its details. This is the same beast that the great Jesuit Le Jeune
witnessed in 1636, caught in a net, and thrown back in horror; the
same beast that controls the terrifying waters of the Great Lakes,
perhaps Superior the most, and sank the *Edmund Fitzgerald*; the
beast that takes our children in particular, to their watery deaths.
Radisson once saw it clinging to the foot of a tree. The fur trader
St. Vincent spotted it in 1782 and never fully recovered. It was,
in his words, about the size of a seven-year-old child. After four
years of searching, Dewdney brought it to some prominence in
1957, having spotted the rock paintings, of course, from a canoe.

His career as a bushman and canoeist can be measured by the
innumerable lakes he paddled, and the portages he clamoured
over. He painted and he painted very well; he wrote two dreadful
novels, thirty years apart, the latter no better than the former; the
element of imagination and of joy in imagination is absent from
his writing, and his fiction suffers fatally from it. Fortunately,
he wrote a memoir, heavily edited it would seem, but a valuable
book — invaluable really — titled *Daylight in the Swamp*, and
published posthumously. It is a book that teems with an irrepress-
ible love of being outdoors and the lore of the outdoors. His life as

a non-Native Canadian incorporates five centuries of European fascination with the Red Man, a fascination that extended from Kafka to Graham Greene and has perhaps contained within it a sort of European revulsion for the world they had created, the feeling of *Europamudigkeit*: a sickness or weariness with Europe, a sense that soon the streets of Europe would once again run with blood. Out of that weariness was born the insatiable desire to know the Native, to touch the Native, to possess, and finally, it would seem, to make a living off the Native.

II

A number of years ago discussing pictographs with a scholarly and effusive Ojibway man who acted as interpreter to the petroglyphs site near Peterborough, I made the mistake of referring to Selwyn Dewdney as the person who "discovered," the Agawa Rock paintings. I had relapsed into the old ways of my Canadian grade-school education that had Columbus "discovering" America as though somehow the millions of people who lived there had forgotten where they put it. It was an unfortunate mistake.

"Hah," snorted the attendant, "Selwyn Dewdney never discovered a thing." Then softening, he added, "Don't get me wrong, I have nothing against *old* Selwyn, it's just I never once saw the man *sober*." He turned to two schoolgirls who had been waiting patiently to question him about Native marriage customs. He explained to them that as a member of the Turtle clan, it would be impossible for him to marry a woman of the Turtle clan. "I just could not do it, don't ask me to explain. It wouldn't be right. It would be like, well, how should I put this...." He thought for a moment and then went on happily putting it to them at great length. The girls were utterly fascinated and it seemed to me that this talkative Ojibway scholar was as much a part of the marketing of the Native as Selwyn Dewdney.

History has been fair to Selwyn. Perhaps it has been too fair and in years to come, Dewdney's efforts will be examined much more skeptically, in particular, his relationship with the troubled alcoholic Cree painter Norval Morrisseau. Selwyn worked uncomfortably hard to turn Morrisseau into a cultural institution; coached, schooled, and prepped him on how to come out into the white urban society of museum administrators and art critics. He instructed him to remove motifs from his paintings, that were not, in Dewdney's view, authentically Indian or Indian enough (a pair of breasts, for example), and was instrumental in fabricating the Woodland School of Art from which Morriseau soon sought to distance himself, calling it nothing but a media creation. In a letter, Dewdney urges him to try "painting on moosehide," and urges him to use colours used by "prehistoric Indians." This practice of Euro-Canadians instructing Native people on how to appear more pure has been seen before; Paul Kane frequently instructed his Native models to change their clothes into what he considered to be more authentic Indian garments — authentic to whom and why are questions that never seem to have entered Dewdney's mind.

For the time being, at least it can be said of Dewdney that he admired and studied Native ways without making the mistake of attempting to become one, and that he managed to get off before the spray-painted Indian maidens with pointy breasts showed up on T-shirts or began belting out songs for the Disney Corporation. Of his own life's work conducted on the oldest rock on the planet, and much of it carried out with his wife, he says simply and profoundly, "we touched an alien culture."

He died in November 1979 following open-heart surgery to correct a faulty valve.

20

Getting a Stone Aroused:
The Life of Robert Markle

On a summer afternoon in the late 1960s, Toronto police officers burst into a top floor of a Yonge Street apartment, looking to apprehend the robber of a Yonge Street bank. Instead they found Robert Markle, wearing large glasses and surrounded by paintings and sketches of nude women. The officers, according to Markle's notebooks, poked about until one of them discovered a pair of binoculars, which he took to the window and aimed at the bank.

"Jesus Christ," he yelled. "I can see the goddamn serial numbers on the vault from here!" Markle, who had been using the binoculars to peep at the mini-skirted legs of the tellers below, answered calmly,

"I'm an artist. I turn the binoculars backward to get a different perspective on my work."

Unsure what to makes of this remark, the police left, but not before one of them turned and waved a finger in Markle's face.

"Smarten up!" he warned.

Fortunately it was too late for that.

* * *

Robert Markle was born in Hamilton, Ontario, in 1936. His father was a "Mohawk in high steel" — the phrase has become common after Joseph Mitchell's 1949 *New Yorker* article and refers to the most glamorous and dangerous job in the construction industry. "Men who want to do it are rare," wrote Mitchell. "Men who *can* do it are rarer." It was agreed this job was best done by Mohawks who "did not have any fear of heights."

Fearful or not, the work was dangerous. A 1907 accident on the Quebec Bridge killed ninety-seven men — thirty-five of them were Mohawks. This danger, combined with long absences from home, defined the working life of men in high steel, including Markle's father, Bruce, who later lost his life in a Buffalo hotel fire while away on a job.

Robert Markle was then nine years old and living in a small house on Barton Street in Hamilton's east end. Directly across the street lay Mahoney Park, where the Mahoney Bears played baseball, and where Markle and his sisters skated on winter mornings. Beyond the outfield fence, a vast industrial landscape stretched to the lake.

Here in this small house on Barton Street began the fascination with the female that would soon define Markle's entire artistic output. In a delightful Christmas memoir appearing in the December 1977 issue of *Toronto Life*, he wrote of this time: "My life was being transformed by my mother's unerring understanding of love." To Markle even Christmas itself was female. The morning was called into existence by his sister, who woke him up, then the visuals of his mother's living room: "The reds, greens, ribbon-golds, purples, soft blues, yellow, half-hidden in amber shadow, dusky under a blazing tree." Finally the gifts. Giving out presents, observed Markle, "was woman's work."

Later his family sat down at a dinner table covered in lace, the tatted and intricate expression of a woman's quiet labour.

This lace, Markle noted, was older than him. Here, in the heart of his mother's home, he received his most meaningful training as an artist. "At my mother's Christmas table," he wrote, "I learned ritual and excellence."

In 1954, the eighteen-year-old left home for Toronto to become, in his words, "a big-time painter." This opportunity, like many in his life, was precipitated by the generosity of women: a scholarship from the Imperial Order Daughters of the Empire.

Robert Markle's swift failure as an art student has come to form the core of a minor legend. Chafing under the strictures of the Art College of Ontario, the frustrated twenty-year-old hurled a bottle of acid against a wall and was promptly expelled. His girlfriend, fellow student, and soon-to-be-his wife and lifelong model, Marlene Shuster, left with him, informing the dean that if he was going to expel Markle, he'd better expel her as well.

What the legend leaves out is a devastated twenty-year-old student writing home to his mother to explain he has been kicked out of art school. In her response, his mother, Kathleen, gently laments Robert's failure to control his emotions, and suggests reasonably that the school had no choice but to expel him. She adds, "I will also be on your side no matter what. You will *never be a failure!*" Her faith was rewarded. In less than ten years her son would become, at least briefly, one of the most discussed and written-about painters in the country.

For a great deal of the twentieth century, the female figure in Canadian painting has existed almost fully clothed beneath the dominance of landscape art and a somewhat puritanical fear of human flesh. In 1931, the Art Gallery of Toronto found it prudent to remove juried works of naked figures from its walls. The Montreal Museum of Fine Arts did the same a decade later. Artist William Brymmer wondered "Why the human body is in such disgrace among us?" Joseph Russell, after twenty years in Paris, returned to Canada and exhibited nudes which, according to art historian Jerrold Morris, were received with "vociferous horror." Artist LeMoine FitzGerald hung a nude over his mantelpiece but took it down after a neighbour complained that her son could see it through the window. The near official dominance of landscape art was confirmed in 1967 when the National Gallery of Canada mounted its three-hundred-year retrospective of Canadian art and went so far as to include *one* nude.

Into this frosty environment strode a young Mohawk determined to turn his talents toward the female figure. Having recently been ousted from the guiding influence of art school, and, more importantly, its life-drawing classes, Markle sought his subject where he could — in the burlesque halls of Yonge Street and Spadina Avenue.

In these smoky rooms, the female body was seen in its power. Here the body was full of movement and agency. "Heroic," Markle called it, erotic and alive. This stands in sharp contrast to the artist's studio model, who is professionally submissive, demure, and whose poses are not her own.

Through the stripper, Markle tackled what is arguably western art's most storied and esteemed subject, expanding the parameters of the nude to include the nudie, the girly picture, the cheesecake, showgirls, the net stocking, the stiletto heel, and the ostrich-feather boa.

Markle was soon light years removed from the east end of Hamilton. He lived in the heart of Toronto, inhaling the

intoxicating scene taking place in the few blocks around Yonge
and Bloor, in Yorkville. The Pornographic Onion; the Mynah Bird
with its stark naked chef; topless dancers; go-go girls in cages;
the Riverboat, the performances there by a young man named
Gordon Lightfoot, soon to become Markle's friend and drinking
companion; The Isaacs Gallery, Rochdale College, free love ...

"I was already an arrogant self-centred prick," wrote Markle.
"But in spite of that I knew I had a lot to learn." That learning
involved a reading of Marshall McLuhan from whom Markle
took the following note: "Open mesh silk stocking is far more
sensuous than the smooth nylon, because the eye must act as a
hand, infilling in and completing the mirage."

In 1965, in a famous raid, the morality police (the "Hogtown
Squad," as Vancouver reporters gleefully called them) removed
Markle's drawings from the Dorothy Cameron Gallery, ensur-
ing Markle's celebrity, and bankrupting one of Canada's most
vibrant outlets for contemporary art. A radio reporter informed
Markle that a judge had ruled that his picture, *Lovers No. 1*,
depicted lesbian activity, which was not allowed. A seething
Markle answered, "Yeah?"

Robert Markle was approaching the status of icon. He was
a member of the Isaac's All-Stars and the Artists' Jazz Band.
He would lend his name to a restaurant called, of course,
Markleangelo's, and be a founding member of Arts' Sake Inc.
He, along with other artists, began teaching at the New School
of Art, the antithesis of the Ontario College of Art — all courses
taught by "practising artists."

As a teacher Markle, invited his students to look hard at their
own drawings and "try to figure out why they're all so shitty."
Afternoon classes were conducted in the Brunswick House

Tavern. Here, according to artist Vera Frenkel, "the conversation was always interesting and sometimes even about art." Also here, in the defining sexism of the Toronto art scene of the 1960s and 1970s, a young Vera Frenkel, following one of Markle's pompous, if not insufferable rants, poured a pitcher of beer over his head and earned his undying respect.

Markle was coming into his own at a time when feminism was called Women's Lib and a feminist was referred to as a Women's Libber. Despite his relentless pursuit of the female nude, he has largely escaped the approbation of feminist criticism and even scrutiny. "What is a feminist to do with Robert Markle?" asked Marjorie Stone at a 1991 Markle retrospective. While observing that Markle's "celebration of female sexuality" usually occurs "somewhere on the border between the erotic and the grotesque," she answers her own question by suggesting that the viewer "participate in the dialogue or polylogue about gender that viewing his work provokes."

The advice is sound, although it is quite possible that Markle would have dismissed it as "another dreary stab at getting one's mental rocks off" — a phrase found in his writings. Despite this predictable pose of anti-intellectualism, Markle was arguably as scholarly, bookish, and as well-educated as any Canadian artist before him or since. It is impossible to be any more intellectual (or succinct) than Markle himself when he addresses the central issue of his own creative process:

> The thing I have most difficulty in dealing with is that distance between outright arousal and the true aspect of perception. I always believe that appeasement of the picture comes before appeasement of myself, but how to explain that seems beyond me. Maybe for the best.

When Markle impersonates Rembrandt on the Global tele-vision show *Witness to Yesterday*, the learning, the confidence, and the arrogance oozes from him. He is utterly convincing as Rembrandt — uncomfortably so, as if Rembrandt were some minor artist attempting to imitate *him*. Markle arrived at the taping with a hangover, was offered coffee, but demanded speed instead, which the studio staff graciously provided. At one point the frus-trated host, Patrick Watson, posed a somewhat windy question to which either Markle or Rembrandt (it is difficult to tell) snapped back, "What are you asking me? Was I a happy man?" Clearly the artist cannot imagine a more contemptible question.

Fortunately these various posturings on the part of Robert Markle do not conceal the work itself: the determined represen-tation of the female forms that invoke de Kooning and Matisse; nature and jazz; the flowing, unexpected lines that can be found in the work of Thelonious Monk, Miles Davis, and Markle's favourite, Lester Young.

Strippers, wrote Markle, especially the good ones, "reach out through the eyes of the audience to get a better look at them-selves." This intriguing observation indicates how deeply he had thought through his artistic project. The link between the viewer and the viewed, the stripper and the customer, is kinetic and fruitful. It is strikingly similar to the patron in an art gallery — reaching out through the eyes of the artist to get a better look at her or himself.

For Markle, this better look demanded sexuality, naked-ness, flesh, skin, and passion. He wrote: "There is a grace in lust that touches on a type of controlled panic." This is where his art exists. Strangely, at the very point where arousal should happen, it usually doesn't. The image refuses to slip into the reassuring safety of pornography; it bolts instead into the unfixable and more dangerous terrain of art. Even Markle's bondage sketches (he called them more accurately "held figures") refuse to deliver the titillation presumed to take place when the unbound and dressed viewer gazes upon the powerless and naked subject. Even in bondage his nudes cannot be held back, they exist strong and unrestrainable. Instead it is the gear of bondage that appears stilted, inorganic, and poorly rendered; the ropes, the straps, the trappings, have no chance against these figures and the power that exudes from them.

In a videotape, "Priceville Prints," Markle can be seen painting the chest of one of his figures. "Exploding tits," he exclaims happily. This coarse and kinetic tendency toward erupting flesh is not unusual in the Markle canon. Strippers, he wrote, "with bombastic bellies," and "women falling, all legs arms, soft flesh, falling through my eyes, my time, falling through my life, sucking my air, touching my mind." For all of this imagery, with its rock-lyric modernity, Markle's nudes also owe a great deal to the muse of nature. They are formed of the landscape, sometimes to such an extent that it's difficult to differentiate between the trunk of a woman and the trunk of a tree. There are paintings in which the branches of a tree are no different from a woman's arms or legs. Both are crooked and alive, both filled with water and living fluid. He paints the bays and inlets of a woman's body, the flowing river bank of the calf and thigh. He immerses her in water, which, on second look, could easily be stage light.

For all of his contemporary indifference toward landscape, Markle's painted nudes are often indistinguishable from the earth, just as the earth is indistinguishable from the nude. In his writing he drives the same point home: "The spun eyes of water ... the softly found summer bronzed flesh ... breasts of polished stone ... winter's white bikini...." In a collage he cuts out the image of a river and turns it into a winding tongue that ends up flowing from a human face. There are times when the nude becomes a branch, a brown stick figure; times when flesh becomes the colour of bark and dirt, and the appendages turn into paws. Calves will suddenly bulge outward, like trees thickening at that point where they touch the ground.

Typically the Markle nude is elevated by the shoe; the ubiquitous stiletto. For Markle, the high heel is the pedestal on which he mounts his inquiry. High heels become a signature, evolving over the years as he himself evolves as an artist. These immense and spindly shoes are the artificial devices that keep her from touching the ground, yet the feet of Markle's nudes are massive and powerful; the shoes have no chance against her. Like the ropes in his bondage sketches, they fail every time. The spiked heels, for all the loving and fetishistic attention they receive, are incapable of disempowering the women who wear them.

"All women," wrote Markle, "remind me of what beauty is." This is the democratic core of his vision and permeates Markle's output, both literary and visual. All women, he insists, (even "the perfumed Rosedale lady lusting") "are the most beautiful women in the world." Markle did not have hangovers, he had "black lace hangovers." In an article on buying a stereo, he recommends the Sure Type 3 diamond needle, because it "caresses and fondles" your records. When he was in his studio working, he was, in his words, painting his wife, recovering and re-loving and redrawing her. In *Priceville Prints*, a confident Harold Klunder blithely says to Markle that his (Klunder's) painting would be no different if he was a woman.

"You don't know that," interjects Markle at once, almost angrily. "You don't know about *the woman part of it!*" Not knowing the woman part of it, that mystery, is the drive behind a great deal of Markle's art. Inherent in the mystery is the dance and the power of human flesh. "As I am aroused," he wrote, "so must they be aroused." Markle was himself fully aware of the moral puritanism that drives the war on pornography. He saw it first-hand when police officers removed his black-and-white female nudes from the walls of the Dorothy Cameron Gallery. He saw it in the moral hysteria that followed the murder of Emmanuel Jacques, a Yonge Street shoeshine boy. "The purge is on," he wrote. "The purge is ugly." The antidote to the purge is a celebration of the erotic, of the naked, human flesh, of undulating kinetic strippers whom Markle called "heroines" and "giants." And to whom his gratitude is palpable.

In *Priceville Prints*, there is an image of Markle, a bolt of grey hair tied behind the back of his head, jowls that overflow his face, large, dark-rimmed glasses and the ubiquitous stained and battered Red Man Chewing Tobacco cap. He is seated at back of the studio directing an electric hair dryer at a lithographic stone. Through the roar he shouts, "I'm just trying to get this stone aroused."

A better summation of Markle is hard to imagine.

As a young man, Robert Markle penetrated the most privileged, the most influential and the most elite art scene in Canada. He did so as a "Native," what he called an "Indian," a Mohawk Indian — the most influential and storied member of the Six Nations Confederacy, a confederacy about which another Mohawk artist, Pauline Johnson, said that no other government existed.

He was born not Markle, but *Maracle*, a name found throughout Six Nations history and today throughout the phone books of southern Ontario. It is suggested that Robert Maracle become Robert Markle at the insistence of his mother, Kathleen, who must have known the burden of Indianhood and was attempting to protect her children from shouldering it, at least in name. In a 1977 letter regarding his Indian status, Robert Markle discovered he was registered as an "Indian" under Band No. 1358, "Band Name: Mohawks of the Bay of Quinte." Not surprisingly, he made this inquiry into his Native status to find out if he qualified for a housing grant.

In today's culture of almost obligatory "identity politics," it is startling to see just how little interest Markle had in exploring or exploiting his Native heritage. There were only three things, insisted Markle, that he never thought about, "being an Indian, fame, and art." Whether he thought about his Native background or not, he was certainly willing to have some fun with it. In the NFB film *Cowboy and Indian*, he is asked, "What part Indian are you?" Markle answers, "The best part." He described himself as "the only Mohawk in North America who was afraid of heights." "If I wasn't Ontario's fattest Indian," he said, "I'd climb that tree." He solemnly insisted that Indians did not sneeze. "What kind of Indian am I?" he wondered out loud. "I don't even like to go outside."

In *Priceville Prints*, Markle was asked if he had been influenced by Indian art, and he answered yes, with a qualification. To Markle it was not his art that was Indian, but the spirit of its creation:

> I'm very interested, naturally, by the things around me. But what I'm really trying to talk about, and this is very dangerous ground, but I know … some … people … whose work is excellent, but they have attitudes about "Once The Work Is Done." … which I don't have. [They] can't wait to stick it upon the wall, to look at it … to get it in a shiny frame and sell it. Even though they make excellent statements as artists,

something else takes over which I think is foreign to an intrinsic aspect of *my culture*, and that's where I see a separation between myself and those people … As I say it's dangerous ground but I sense it as something that is close to the spiritual.

"Good or bad," he said, what he truly appreciated is that the effort was being made to keep the river flowing.

In paintings, in beadwork, in his whirligigs, his fence sculptures, his baseball uniforms, his essays, articles, poems, his keyboard-playing, his tenor saxophone, his liner notes, his book covers, his neon sculptures, and his friendships, Robert Markle was determined to keep the river flowing.

On a clear July night in 1990, coming home from the Mount Royal Tavern, in Mount Forest, Ontario, he drove his car into the back end of a tractor and was killed. He was fifty-three years old.

More Dundurn Books about Interesting Canadian Folk

100 Canadian Heroines
Famous and Forgotten Faces
Merna Forster
978-1550025149
$24.99

100 Canadian Heroines profiles some remarkable women; from the adventurous Gudridur the Viking to murdered Mi'kmaq activist Anna Mae Aquash. You'll meet heroines in science, sport, preaching and teaching, politics, war and peace, arts and entertainment, et cetera. The book is full of amazing facts and fascinating trivia about intriguing figures like mountaineer Phyllis Munday, activist Hide Shimizu, Arctic guide Tookoolito, unionist Lea Roback, movie mogul Mary Pickford, and singer Portia White. Great quotes and photos are featured in this inspiring collection. Discover some of the many heroines Canada can be proud of. Find out how we're remembering them.

100 More Canadian Heroines
Famous and Forgotten Faces
Merna Forster
978-1554889709
$24.99

In this second installment of the bestselling Canadian Heroines series, author Merna Forster brings together 100 more incredible stories of great characters and wonderful images. Meet famous and forgotten women in fields such as science, sport, politics, war and peace, and arts and entertainment, including the original Degrassi kids, Captain Kool, hockey star Hilda Ranscombe, and the woman dubbed "the atomic mosquito." This book is full of amazing facts and trivia about extraordinary women. You'll learn about Second World War heroine Joan Fletcher Bamford, who rescued 2,000 Dutch captives from a prison camp in a Sumatran jungle while commanding seventy Japanese soldiers. Hilwie Hamdon was the woman behind the building of Canada's first mosque, and Frances Gertrude McGill was the crime fighter named the "Sherlock Holmes of Saskatchewan." Read on and discover 100 more Canadian heroines and how they've changed our country.

Breakthrough!
Canada's Greatest Inventions and Innovations
John Melady
978-1459708525
$19.99

Canadians are behind a variety of cutting-edge products, life-saving medicines, innovative machines, and fascinating ideas. Although our inventions have typically been created with little fanfare, financing, or expectation of return, they have often gone on to play important roles in day-to-day life. Our "greatest invention" is probably insulin, which millions of people depend on for life and health. But the light bulb, the Canadarm, and the BlackBerry certainly vie for that honour as well. Some of our inventions are small: the paint roller, the Robertson screwdriver, and the crash position indicator — the forerunner of the black box on planes. Others are larger: the jetliner, the snow-blower, and the snowmobile. Some, such as Standard Time, are really just complex ideas while others, such as the pacemaker, are triumphs of complex technology. Put simply, Canadians are supremely innovative!

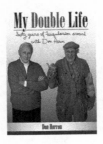

My Double Life
Sexty Yeers of Farquharson Around with Don Harn
Don Harron
978-1459705500
$35.00

After fifteen books about somebody else (mostly alter ego Charlie Farquharson) plus one book by his drag-queen character, Charlie's rich city cousin Valerie Rosedale, Don Harron now presents the story of his seventy-seven-year stint in the entertainment business. The actor's colourful career includes such highlights as making money in 1935 as a ten-year-old cartoonist doing mother-and-son banquets; winning an ACTRA Award as best radio host for *Morningside*; six stage shows on Broadway, three in London's West End, and ten years of Shakespeare in three countries; a Gemini Award for lifetime achievement; writing the lyrics for five musicals, including *Anne of Green Gables*; and being appointed to the Canadian Country Music Hall of Honours due to his appearances on *Hee Haw*. Whether playing a serious stage role or hamming it up as Charlie Farquharson, Harron is always insightful and provides a unique perspective on a long life in the entertainment business.

Eleven Out of Ten
The Life and Work of David Pecaut
Helen Burstyn
978-1459707924
$35.00

City builder David Pecaut has been called a visionary and a pragmatist, passionate and compassionate, a bridge builder, a catalyst, and a trailblazer. Though David was a business leader and management consultant, most of these accolades flow from his volunteer work as a civic entrepreneur. When Toronto was in the doldrums because of the SARS scare, David helped the city restore its tourism industry by chairing the Toronto3 Alliance, launched by a flamboyant Rolling Stones concert. David was perhaps best known for co-founding Luminato, the international festival that each spring showcases the world's finest artists to audiences of over a million. As chair of the Toronto City Summit Alliance, David worked as easily with the homeless, minorities, and poverty activists as with billionaires, corporate CEOs, and labour leaders to tackle pressing social and economic issues. David's efforts to make Toronto the most socially and culturally dynamic urban centre in the world were cut short when he succumbed to cancer in December 2009. When it became obvious that his time was running out, he took copious notes and recorded interviews with friends, colleagues, and family, all of which are the basis for this book, a memoir by his wife Helen Burstyn.

The Secret of the Blue Trunk
Lise Dion; translated by Liedewy Hawke
978-1459704510
$21.99

In this true story, Armande Martel, a young nun from Quebec, is arrested by the Germans in 1940 during a stay at her religious order's mother house in Brittany. She spends the war years in a German concentration camp. After her return to Canada, she leaves the Church, finds the love of her life in Montreal, and adopts Lise Dion. Growing up, Lise is familiar with only a few facts of her mother's past. It's when she clears her mother's small apartment after her death that Lise Dion discovers the key to the blue trunk, which was always locked. This key unlocks the mystery of Armande's early life, and Lise decides to write *The Secret of the Blue Trunk*.